REVIEWS FOR:

Emmanuel

I have known Andrea Miller since she was in sixth grade, and she has always been a devoted disciple of our Lord Jesus. She has experienced numerous miracles in her life and now lives to bless others through her profound love and humble service to God and His children. *Emmanuel* is a true reflection of Andrea's beautiful life of faith, hope and love, and her desire to draw others closer to God. Her thoughtful insights into Scripture passages are extremely inspiring, and her love for God and His children is strongly evident in her book. By adding her own personal reflections, Andrea encourages the readers to walk our Christian journey to our Heavenly Kingdom with the Lord Jesus, holy heroes, and saints. *Emmanuel* is a splendid gift to the readers, a precious treasure of spiritually uplifting book. May God use Andrea's book to draw the readers closer to Jesus, our Lord and Savior.

—Sr. Tresa Jose, FCC.

***

Andrea Miller has always put others and their challenges ahead of her own. While her own have been formidable, they convinced her at an early age that her life was in the hands of her Savior. She seems to have been guided by God. Andrea's knowledge of the Bible is awesome, but her ability to explain the meaning of the Bible's words to touch the hearts of everyday people is her talent. We are inspired by the wisdom she displays...and she tells us, "They are not my words; they are God's word."

She walks the talk of "loving her neighbors" by raising funds for those less fortunate and by sharing her wisdom through this book of Bible-based devotionals. This book is a gift for everyone who would like to walk with Andrea and her God.

She is a treasure for us.

—Chip & Nancy Roach.

***

Andrea Miller is an amazing young woman. She reads Scripture with a child-like faith, but then goes deeper, asks questions, studies, seeking deeper meaning. Her insights are often astounding. She has an earnestness to learn all she can about God, then lives that out with refreshing openness and vulnerability. She does not pretend to have all the answers; she seeks all the answers.

i

Andrea's writings are a gift to anyone who also seeks insight and deeper meaning. She is honest and authentic; truly a gifted child of God with a higher purpose. This book is an invitation to take a walk with the Lord.

You will seek me and find me when you seek me with all your heart.
—Jeri 29:13.

—**Rev. Larry Marshall**, Pastor, Captiva Chapel by the Sea.

***

Andrea Miller was a shy sixth grader the first time I met her more than twenty years ago. Today, I am honored to call her a friend. Andrea is a walking miracle, something I have never said about another human being. What Andrea has survived and overcome, and what she has done with the talents and the time the Lord have given her, overwhelm and humble me. I noticed when Andrea was still in middle school that she had the spirit of a saint (her empathy and compassion) and the heart of a lion (her actions on behalf of those in need). Now she has channeled her efforts into a reflection on the Scriptures. Andrea's book *Emmanuel* is encouraging, insightful, genuine, and for this Christian, convicting. You, too, will be challenged and encouraged (and maybe even a little humbled) in your walk with our Lord when you read *Emmanuel.* The read is a journey worth taking.

— **Tim Wortman**, English teacher.

***

I first met Andrea when I was serving as Pastor at Chapel by the Sea on Captiva Island, Florida. Andrea is a person of great spiritual depth who feels the power and presence of God in her life both on the mountain tops of joy and in the valley of deep shadows. Her words here convey her deep faith and commitment to a God who loves each and every one of us. In the words of an old prayer, my hope is that you will "read, mark and inwardly digest" what she has written here.

—**Rev John Cedarleaf,** Pastor, *United Church of Christ.*

Emmanuel

Satisfying the Thirsty Soul

Andrea Miller

Published by KHARIS PUBLISHING, an imprint of KHARIS MEDIA LLC.

Copyright © 2021 Andrea Miller

ISBN-13: 978-1-63746-027-6
ISBN-10: 1-63746-027-9

Library of Congress Control Number: 2021930558

All KHARIS PUBLISHING products are available at special quantity discounts for bulk purchase for sales promotions, premiums, fund-raising, and educational needs. For details, contact:

Kharis Media LLC
Tel: 1-479-599-8657

support@kharispublishing.com
www.kharispublishing.com

CONTENTS

Introduction

And they will call him Emmanuel, which is 'God with us.'
—Matthew 1:23

From beginning to end, the Holy Word speaks of God's love for His people. It is a grave loss if we misunderstand His Word and thus the love and forgiveness He offers us. Reading is vain if we desire nothing more than to skim the pages, taking His teachings and hiding them in our mind, desiring not to learn from them, to act on them, to grow stronger in faith from the truths He sets forth.

Scanning the pages of God's Word does not make one God's child, nor sets the sinner free. God's desire is for His people to flourish. He means to educate and strengthen, uplift and grow. May we learn the truths of His character, to confirm being shaped to the image of His child. God desires the whole heart; we may give it to Him by communion with Him through His Holy Word. "But be doers of the word, and not merely hearers who deceive themselves" (James 1:22). Don't just read the Bible…live it!

Before the silver cord is snapped, and the golden bowl is broken, and the pitcher is broken at the fountain, and the wheel broken at the cistern, and the dust returns to the earth as it was, and the breath returns to God who gave it. Vanity of vanities, says the Teacher; all is vanity. —Ecclesiastes 12:6-8

King Solomon portrays in this chapter the value of being conscious of our sins against our Creator and repenting of them, thus seeking forgiveness. As time passes, the one that takes pleasure only in carnal desires, striving not for the higher goal and truths given by our Maker through His grace and love will be loath to regret their sins, finding only remorse and regret in their lack of repentance.

There will be nothing to cherish, for all will be gone: "the dust returns to the earth" (vs. 7) as it was first created. The soul will thirst and not be satisfied; for all that satisfied was to acquire earthly gain. That is why King Solomon asks us to repent while we still can: to put aside earthly treasures and look to a higher goal, realizing our sinfulness, lusts, and greed, laying them at the feet of God, desiring to follow Him; for soon our bodies will return to dust, and the soul within will return to God. What then do we have to say on that day of God's wrath when he judges the nations? What excuse will we plead for denying Him all our earthly lives? We will be guilty before the throne of our maker. Repent. Repent while there is still breath to do so, and come close to God.

Chapter 1

The Beginning of Days

Then God said, 'Let there be light.' — **Genesis 1:3**

The first thing wrought in the soul is light. The light has been dimmed and darkened by the fall of man, blinding humanity to understanding God and His love for us. Darkness would have always been upon the fallen man if the Son of God had not "come and given us understanding" (1John 5:20). By His love and grace, we become light in the Lord. As God separates the light from the dark, so too does He separate the light of the soul from the darkness of sin, if only by His grace and guidance of His Holy Spirit. May we seek after His Spirt, finding the light always through Christ the Lord.

But the land that you are crossing over to occupy is a land of hills and valleys, watered by rain from heaven, a land that the Lord your God looks after. The eyes of the Lord your God are always on it, from the beginning to the end of the year. —Deuteronomy 11:11-12

Today we stand at the threshold of the unknown. Sorrows and defeats may await us; yet blessings of peace, joy, and strength may follow not far behind.

Just as the land God gave to the Israelites was a land with hills and valleys, so too will our future be. The valleys would not thrive without the hills that take the rain from Heaven to water the earth, and so it is with our heart; our faith would not be washed in the blessings flowing from our Maker if the road was nothing but smooth and level ground. Sorrows, doubts, or momentary defeats may be waiting at the door -these are the mountains and hills we are to climb-. Yet with a faithful heart, we can look upward receiving the blessings of joy, peace, and strength that God gives to each of us: His "rain from Heaven."

Just as "the eyes of the Lord your God are always on it" (vs. 12), so too does the Lord always have His eyes on each of His people, from the beginning to the end of their days.

> ***Then the eyes of both were opened, and they knew that they were naked; and they sewed fig leaves together and made loincloths for themselves.*** —Genesis 3:7

Through the grace of God, Adam and Eve's eyes were opened to the nakedness of their souls. Stripped of happiness, they saw a loving God provoked and His grace and favor forfeited. They were stripped of that honor and glory, the privilege and power with which they were vested and lost the image of God that was upon them. That robe of purity, innocence, and righteousness with which they were arrayed was also lost, and they found themselves naked and defenseless, unable to screen themselves from the curses of righteous law and the fury of cruel justice. By God's grace, our eyes are spiritually opened when we sin. In many ways we are conscious of the nakedness of our soul, taking for granted the blessings God has bestowed upon us, turning from His commands to follow some lust or lie, and losing the communion we once had with our Maker.

Often, we try harder to run from our sin than to repent of it. We cover our sinfulness, as Adam and Eve did -not with fig leaves- but by denial of ever having done something wrong, skipping over our faults, as if they never occurred at all, or casting the blame on someone else, as Eve did (vs. 13). Let us not run from our sin, for soon it will catch up to us once again and prove itself an even deeper hurt to our soul than when we had committed it. Our Lord gives us His grace and favor that we may come to Him, repenting of our ways, and asking Him for the wisdom to overcome the wicked temptations that lead us into sinful acts, pleading, not for pardon but the guidance of the Holy Spirit, that we may be lead in holiness.

Brothers and sisters, we need not focus on our sin, but rather on the One who overcame the world of wickedness and sin, triumphing over death and the eternal damnation of the ones who oppose God's wrath. Let us be washed in His blood, renewed every morning to know that the Spirit guides us, always away from sin to redemption.

He will strike your head, and you will strike his heel. —Genesis 3:15

Heaven and hell can never be reconciled, nor light and darkness; no more can Satan be reconciled to a sanctified soul. There is a continual struggle between the wicked and the godly in this world. A gracious promise is here made of Christ as the Deliverer of fallen man from the power of Satan. Here was the dawn of the Gospel day: no sooner was the wound given than the remedy was provided and revealed. Great encouragement this should give to sinners, knowing that our Savior became the very "bone of our bone" (Genesis 2:23) that He may make amends for the fatal blow of the serpent. Christ's sufferings and death pointed at in Satan's bruising His heel. And Christ's sufferings are continued in the sufferings of the saints for His name. The Devil tempts them, persecutes and slays them and so strikes the heel of Christ, who is afflicted in their afflictions. But while the heel is bruised on earth, the Head of Satan shall be struck by the victory of Christ. Christ baffled Satan's temptations and rescued souls out of Satan's hands. By His death, He gave a fatal blow to the Devil's kingdom: a wound to the head of this serpent that cannot be healed. As the Gospel gains ground and points more souls to the object of their faith -Christ's resurrection- the more Satan's defeat becomes evident.

Then the Lord said, 'My spirit shall not abide in mortals forever. — Genesis 6:3

By the breath of God's Spirit, human life was sustained on the earth (Genesis 2:7, 7:22). Each, in turn, is subject to this breath, as from it we came. God being Spirit and humans being flesh, God's sinless Spirit could no longer abide in or wrestle with man, who had corrupted the power, humility, and holiness of the soul in order to satisfy the desires of the body, no longer desiring to carry out the will of God. He would not allow His Spirit to uplift and maintain a sinful people. He would leave them to be hardened in sin and ripened to destruction. The one that hates to be reformed by the grace of God is the one that will be punished by the justice of God. But the one that comes to repentance is the one looked upon by God with favor, the one that God will yet sustain by His Spirit.

As he walked by the Sea of Galilee, he saw two brothers, Simon, who is called Peter, and Andrew his brother, casting a net into the sea - for they were fishermen-. And he said to them, 'Follow me, and I will make you fish for people.' Immediately they left their nets and followed him. —Matthew 4:18-20

When Christ began to preach, He began to gather disciples who would be hearers and afterwards preachers of His doctrine, who would be witnesses of His miracles and afterwards testify concerning them. Notice the word *immediately*. Peter and Andrew did not pause to ask questions of Jesus; they obeyed without hesitation. We read on to find James and John *immediately* obeying the call of Christ (vs. 21-22). When Christ speaks to our heart by the Holy Spirit, we too must obey without hesitation. When we obey, Christ begins to bless; immediate response to Christ's calling results in immediate action on His part. Diligence in an honest calling is pleasing to Christ, and it is no hindrance to a holy life. When Christ calls, those who follow without delay are the ones who rise with Him above the temptations of this world.

3

Like Christ, we too can be fishers of people; like the men He sent forth to gather disciples, we too can cast the net of faith into the sea of wandering souls, if nothing else but by the power and guidance of the Holy Spirit.

Chapter 2

Communion with the Maker

Jacob was left alone; and a man wrestled with him until daybreak.
— **Genesis 32:24**

Being alone, Jacob more fully spread his fears before the Lord in prayer. While he prayed, one in the likeness of a man -the second person of the Holy Trinity -met him there and wrestled with his heart. When the Spirit helps our infirmities, and our earnest and vast desires can scarcely find words to utter them, and we still mean more than we can express, then prayer is indeed wrestling with God. When God wrestles with our heart, we are forced from our fears to focus on Him. We fall into His arms and rely on Him alone; our spirit is brought into the courtroom of Christ to commune with Him. However, tried or discouraged, we shall prevail, and prevailing with God in prayer, we shall prevail against all enemies that strive with us. Having power with God, we shall have power with man, also. Those who would have the blessing of Christ must resolve to take no denial. The earnest prayer is the effectual prayer.

A lasting mark of honor is put upon Jacob when his name is changed to Israel (vs. 28). Those are truly honorable who are mighty in prayer. The sun rose on Jacob (vs. 31): it is sunrise of the soul which has had communion with God. We too will experience the spiritual blessings from the Lord, if only we would seek to commune with Him and prevail in prayer. The way to get spiritual blessings is to wrestle with God in prayer. The way to get earthly blessings is to refer ourselves to God concerning them. The one who truly understands the power of prayer will strive to understand the power of God.

He withdrew from there in a boat to a deserted place by himself. —
Matthew 14:13

After hearing of the death of John the Baptist, Jesus was greatly grieved. Drawing Himself aside for a time, He fixed His eyes solely on the Father. Our heavenly Father calls us aside from our work for a season to be with Him. Away from the demands of life, we too can fix our eyes solely on our heavenly Father, watching, waiting, and praying, while He reveals further acts of His grace to us. Our mind is quietened as we listen to His voice speak softly to us.

God's voice demands the silence of our heart; He speaks to us when there is no inner storm.[1]

During these times of seclusion, we are shown deeper levels of knowledge, love, and grace by our heavenly Father. Lessons are learned of His tenderness; in turn, humbling our heart for greater work for Him. It is not surprising that after this small time of seclusion, Jesus performed the beautiful act of feeding the five thousand (Matthew 14:16-21). His heart was humbled by their need, and the Father's deeper grace that Jesus was shown shined even brighter. God prepares us for miraculous acts, showing His deeper love, compassion, and grace to a downcast world; but first He must draw us aside for a time to be alone with Him; then, with a humbled heart and stronger faith we can move forward, proclaiming His love.

He said to me, 'Do not fear, Daniel, for from the first day that you set your mind to gain understanding and to humble yourself before your God, your words have been heard, and I have come because of your words.'—Daniel 10:12

The prayer from a sincere heart never falls on deaf ears. In response to Daniel's words, God was glad to hear his prayer, answering him, but by His own timing.

From the very first day we begin to look toward God, He is ready to meet us in mercy, and hear our prayer. The Lord is quick in hearing the fervent prayer of a humble soul, though He does not presently let us know it. Our prayers are heard by our Maker even when a response does not come in the timing we wish. A soul that would obtain great things from God by prayer must be solemn and fervent, constantly seeking Him. Faithful prayer sends blessings from heaven to save.

Then Elisha prayed: 'O Lord, please open his eyes that he may see.' So, the Lord opened the eyes of the servant, and he saw; the mountain was full of horses and chariots of fire all around Elisha.—2 Kings 6:17

When the enemies of God and the Church of Christ find themselves ready to triumph, they will find themselves conquered and triumphed over. The greatest kindness we can do for those who are fainthearted is to pray for them, to commend them to the great power of God's grace. Elisha prayed for his people, but he prayed that their eyes would be spiritually opened. What

---

[1] George Mathesen. (1895). *Searching in the Silence*. Castle and Company, revised (2018).

6

Elisha saw around him was not the massive army of the Syrians but an army of angels, horses, and chariots of fire. Elisha's eyes were opened to see heaven poured out before him and God's army sent to fight against the enemy. He wished for his servant to see what he saw: the grace of God poured out. Elisha also prayed that the enemy would be spiritually blinded: they saw, but they did not perceive. It is for this two-fold judgment that Christ came down to this earth -seeking to spiritually open our eyes to the truth of God's love, mercy, and grace, that we may no more be blind-.

Our faith will make fools of the enemy, if only we hold our victory always in the Lord. We will be empowered with divine goodness and divine power -power poured out by God when His children call on His name-. Opening our eyes will be the silencing of our fears. When our eyes are spiritually opened, we will see the sovereignty and power of Heaven, and the less we will fear the calamities of this earth. May our eyes always be opened to the spiritual truths that God reveals to us.

> **For everyone who asks receives, and everyone who searches finds, and for everyone who knocks, the door will be opened.** — Luke 11:10

Do not misunderstand what Jesus was trying to teach His apostles. We cannot simply ask for what we desire according to our sinful heart and carnal desires. We must seek what is spiritually revealed to us through the Holy Spirit. James reminds us, "You ask and do not receive, because you ask wrongly, in order to spend what you get on your pleasures" (James 4:3). We ask for what will bring pleasure to our self and not to God. We must have the right ends in view: what will bring God glory. Christ encourages fervency and constancy in prayer. We must come for that which is needful. God may not answer our prayer speedily, yet He will answer in due time if we continue to pray.

Observe what to pray for; we must ask for the Holy Spirit. By asking for the Holy Spirit, we invite God to dwell in our heart, and we begin to understand the heart of God. We must pray fervently and sincerely, seek diligently, and continue to approach the throne of God's grace, knocking at His mercy-seat; we will be blessed when the door does open.

> **Elijah was a human being like us, and he prayed fervently that it might not rain, and for three years and six months it did not rain on the earth.** — James 5:17

James was stating a perfect example to the previous verse: "The prayer of the righteous is powerful and effective" (vs. 16); Elijah was that perfect example. We must, like Elijah, have an innermost prayer life. Elijah dwelled in prayer; he prayed with much earnestness, with great vehemence and intensity of spirit. We must keep praying. Faithful prayer cuts us off from everything but God. In 1 Kings, we read: "So Ahab went up to eat and to drink. Elijah went up to the top of Carmel; there he bowed himself down upon the earth and put his face between his knees" (18:42). We must let our faith -not our sight- guide our prayer life. Elijah prayed for God to send a drought on the earth, and God answered his prayer. Why should we doubt that God can do powerful things in response to our prayers? We're not relying on some power within our self, nor conjuring magic; we're asking God, and He is the One who is acting.

When a righteous person, a true believer justified in Christ and by His grace walking before God in holy obedience, presents an effectual and fervent prayer, wrought in his heart by the power of the Holy Spirit, raising holiness and believing expectations and so leading earnestly to plead the promises of God at His mercy-seat, it avails much. It's enough to simply utter words; we must be fervent in prayer. Thoughts must be fixed, desires must be firm and ardent, and graces exercised. This instance of the power of prayer encourages every Christian to be earnest in prayer.

Why are you cast down, O my soul, and why are you disquieted within me? Hope in God; for I shall again praise him, my help and my God. —Psalm 42:5

As though he were two men, the psalmist talks to himself, mingling his own doubts and grief with God's love and grace. His faith reasons with his fears; his hope argues with his sorrows. There may be times we, like David, ask God, "Why have you forgotten me?" (vs. 9) But we must turn as David did and again proclaim our hope in God (vs. 11). There is never a time when we cannot pour out our heart to the Lord, as David did. Forgetting this promise, our soul is cast down, causing us to forget our God, the *living* God. An emptiness lies within us that can only be filled by the Lord. Letting our troubles triumph over us, we fail to sing the song of truth in our heart that God triumphs always over our troubles. May we praise Him for His abundant love and grace. Let us never think that the God of our life and the Rock of our salvation has forgotten us if we have made His mercy, truth, and power our refuge.

Everything may always be brought to God "by prayer and petition, with thanksgiving" (Philippians 4:6). And in all of our times of need, we may exercise our faith through the power and love of God. Whatever our need or however great our difficulties, we must humble our heart before the Lord and like a child, thank Him for the hope He gives us. More prayer, more exercising of faith, and more patient waiting will lead to abundant blessings;

8

and there will never be a time that we will be downcast. Our soul will be eternally uplifted, rooted in the firm ground of God's love.

All things can be done for the one who believes. —Mark 9:23

Nothing comes to us simply by asking. God means to teach us faith, namely the trial of faith, the discipline of faith, the patience of faith, and the courage of faith. These lessons will lead us to our goal: victorious faith. Through the trials and hardships in life, our faith is strengthened. With strengthened faith, we will rest in the peace of God's Word, even before any physical evidence of an answer comes to us. Like any disciplined child, God must teach us the type of faith that means to carry out His purpose and will, not our own. Just as David reminds us, "Commit your way to the Lord; trust in him, and he will act" (Psalm 37:5).

Patient faith is waiting on God's timing, not our own. When we listen for the voice of the Holy Spirit whispering His answer in our heart, we learn to be patient, remaining content, and yet, have no physical evidence of His answer. Courageous faith has the ability to face difficulties, danger, and pain, knowing that God holds our life in place, exactly where it's meant to be. Obtaining the goal of victorious faith, prayer no longer becomes a job but a conversation with our Heavenly Father. Like any good listener, He will come to our side and open both ears wide, listening in gladness to what we have to say, be it good or ill. We no longer need physical evidence to come right away. God replies our sincere prayers by speaking His response gently in our heart; then when the physical evidence of His answer does come, we will thank Him a hundredfold. Trial of faith, discipline of faith, patience of faith, courage of faith… eventually lead us to the victory of faith!

'Go; your son will live.' The man believed the word that Jesus spoke to him and started on his way. — John 4:50

Without seeing any physical sign that his son would live, the official faithfully took Jesus at His word. He planted his faith in the spiritual answer to his request without seeing an immediate answer to his plea. If we are confronted with a circumstance that demands immediate prayer, we must pray in such a way that we believe God and can thank Him for the answer. In His good timing, He will whisper the answer in our heart. We may not see the external answer immediately; we must not pray in such a way that shows our demanding and discomfort to have the request answered. This type of prayer is clearly self-wrought prayer and the work of the enemy; our faith will be weakened and prayer will become a hindrance rather than a help. Such prayers only show the unrest of our heart and unrest implies unbelief.

9

May we watch and pray so that we will not fall into the temptation to pray for our desired results. Prayer will never slow down or speed up God's timing; we must pray in such a way that shows our faith, not our haste. When God reveals His answer to us and whispers it softly into our heart, we will enter a state of calm rest. It's painful waiting to see what the next day will hold, but deep in our heart, we hear the answer, again and again. When God's answer is fully rooted in our heart, we know the peace of the Spirit. We still pray, thanking God for His answer, but each day that dawns is no more a hindrance in the road; all we see is Christ holding our hand, walking with us through it all. Then, when it is time for us to receive the physical evidence of His answer, we can't stop thanking Him enough for it.

> *Asa cried to the Lord his God, 'O Lord, there is no difference for you between helping the mighty and the weak. Help us, O Lord our God, for we rely on you, and in your name, we have come against this multitude. O Lord, you are our God; let no mortal prevail against you.'* —2 Chronicles 14:11

In the storms of life, we must plead to the Master! Often, we should remind ourselves of His awesome power, His unmatchable strength, and His unending grace to stand before His children and their enemies. Many times, life's circumstances seem very much against us. In Asa's case, he stood against one million men and three hundred chariots (vs. 9). Asa had no choice but to turn and look up to God. When life's circumstances are very much against us, we too need to look up. We need to remember that the very real, living God stands between us and the enemy. Sometimes our Heavenly Father does not turn to us until we turn to Him, reminding us that He is the only one that can beat the odds (Isaiah 30:18). Asa and his army beat the odds against the huge army of the Ethiopians. And we too will beat the odds of life if we but only look up to God.

> *Give ear to my prayer, O God; do not hide yourself from my supplication. Attend to me and answer me; I am troubled in my complaint. I am distraught.* —Psalm 55:1-2

Why does the Lord seem to hear some prayers yet not others? Perhaps it could be in the way we pray? Desperate prayer leads only to destruction and comes not from the heart; it shows our worry, our fear, and our eagerness to be heard by someone. The prayer from the sincere heart never falls on deaf ears. Let us pray to our Maker because we desire communion with Him. We desire to be heard by none other than God Himself and pour out our heart to no one else but Christ. Let us pray in a way that shows our faith, not our fear: this is the prayer our Father accepts as genuine, steadfast, and true: the prayer our Maker opens His ears to.

> *If you abide in me, and my words abide in you, ask for whatever you wish, and it will be done for you.* —John 15:7

This does not pave the way for selfish ambition where we only want to come to Christ for the valued desires which we lack to be fulfilled. This must be understood not of temporal things -riches, honor, profits, pleasures, or whatever the carnal mind of a believer may sometimes desire-, but of things spiritual, and with such limitations and restrictions as these: whatever is "according to the will of God" (1 John 5:24), whatever is for the glory of God, whatever compliments our own spiritual profit and edification, and whatever is agreeable to the words and doctrines of Christ. Everything of this kind may be asked in faith, and with a submission to the Divine will, we may expect to receive.

> *You have wrapped yourself with a cloud so that no prayer can pass through.* —Lamentations 3:44

Despite the prophet's mourning over the people's sins and transgressions against God, he yet finds hope for them to return to the Lord. Sometimes the only way to get through to His people is for God to shut Himself out, to veil Himself in a cloud, as to hide His face. When sin is not pardoned, God is forced to show His wrath and anger, as He cannot let sin escape unheeded. Later in the third chapter, Jeremiah proclaims "you heard my plea" (vs. 56) and, "You came near when I called on you; you said, 'Do not fear!'" (vs. 57). We look up to God for deliverance; He looks down from Heaven and hears our cry. Do we see and understand so deeply our sins and false acts against God that they pierce our heart and bring pain to our soul? Then may the hour come for our heart to cry out to God for deliverance.

> *Therefore confess your sins to one another, and pray for one another, so that you may be healed. The prayer of the righteous is powerful and effective.* —James 5:16

Sisters and brothers in Christ make up Christ's church. As sisters and brothers of one family, we must uplift and strengthen our fellow believers. It is necessary to exercise faith and hope under afflictions; prayer is the appointed means for obtaining and increasing the grace of the Lord.

Acknowledging our faults to one other will tend greatly to peace and brotherly love, not only humbling our own heart of our sinfulness and need of grace but humbling the hearts of those who -like us- need the very same grace. To pray for one another in sincerity, binding our faith to that of our

11

fellow believer, creates an even stronger alliance to stand against Satan and the darkness of fear and doubt. When our brothers and sisters are weakened in battle, we show God's grace by standing for them. As one family, we certainly ought to fight against a common enemy, helping the weakened rise again.

While Peter was kept in prison, the church prayed fervently to God for him. —Acts 12:5

It is not surprising that when Peter was imprisoned, the whole Church felt his pain. Brothers and sisters in Christ are one family. When one hurts, we all hurt; and when one is afflicted, we all are afflicted.

The Church of Christ had no other refuge but to turn to God in earnest prayer. There is no other refuge in times of danger; God hears the sincere prayer even in times of discouraging circumstances. Prevalent, intense, ardent, and sincere prayer is the type sisters and brothers need to lift up to the Lord. The author uses the term "fervently"; the church prayed with intense emotion for Peter, without ceasing. When an awful danger, damage, or circumstance plagues our brothers and sisters, it is no surprise that the faithful in Christ would learn the true value and meaning of soul-felt prayer.

Then Jesus told them a parable about their need to pray always and not to lose heart. —Luke 18:1

Earnest steadiness in prayer will bring about spiritual blessings. Perseverance in prayer leads to strengthened faith and power to overcome Satan's nets of fear and doubt. From Genesis to the end of the New Testament, there are many examples of Christ's children persisting in prayer. The earnest prayer is pleasing to God. The widow prayed consistently, never losing heart, thus prevailing over her enemies; and when we prevail with God in prayer, we prevail over man, also (Genesis 32:28). God blesses our tenacious faith. We must pray and never grow weary of it. By beginning a prayer and failing to see it through to the end, we ensnare our soul in webs of doubt. As soon as we see that our petition has not been fulfilled, we give up. The prayer from God's children that is stopped early in its tracks is the prayer that is never heard by God. Persistent prayer is prevailed prayer. Seeking God's face will not be in vain if only we would strive to continue praying and not give up on God.

Until now you have not asked for anything in my name. Ask and you will receive, so that your joy may be complete. —John 16:24

Asking in Christ's name is acknowledging our unworthiness to receive anything from the Father and shows our full dependence upon Christ as the Lord of our righteousness.

The frequency with which Jesus enforces offering up petitions in His name shows that the great end of the reflection of Christ is to impress us with a deep sense of our sinfulness and of the merit and power of His death, whereby we have access to the Father. When Christ died, "The curtain of the temple was torn in two" (Matthew 27:51). He alone opened the way to the Father. To acknowledge the Father in the name of Christ is to confess that the two are one and the need to come to the Father by the person of Jesus Christ. All joy we have takes its root in the person of Jesus Christ; our joy is complete only in and through Him.

> *Do not worry about anything, but in everything by prayer and supplication with thanksgiving let your requests be made known to God. And the peace of God, which surpasses all understanding, will guard your hearts and your minds in Christ Jesus.*
> —Philippians 4:6-7

Paul contrasts anxiety and prayer by putting a fine line between the two. The key to less anxiety is more prayer. The more we spend in time of communion with the Lord, the less anxiety and worry will come upon our heart. When we bring our worries and set them at the feet of Christ, His peace overpowers the worry we once felt. This peace is deserving of none other than our complete adoration and praise; the peace that comes only from God, that "surpasses *all* understanding." This is Paul's request to the Philippians and to each of his readers: that we come to Christ with that which we count as worry. As an additive to our supplication, Paul asks that we remember our praise and adoration to our Maker; and when sincere prayer reaches the throne of Christ, He gives us the Spirit of peace which will be with us always (vs. 9).

> *When they had prayed, the place in which they were gathered together was shaken; and they were all filled with the Holy Spirit and spoke the word of God with boldness. Now the whole group of those who believed were of one heart and soul, and no one claimed private ownership of any possessions, but everything they owned was held in common. With great power, the apostles gave their testimony to the resurrection of the Lord Jesus, and great grace was upon them all.* —Acts 4:31-33

The prayer of the apostles shook the very ground of Heaven, that their faith would be established and sound. The Holy Spirit was sent from above

13

to fill their souls with the very Words of Christ. Their prayer was so bold that the apostles felt the power of the Spirit, the evidence of sense confirming an inward, spiritual consciousness. The very language of the Holy Spirit became present in each of them, and they began to speak in Tongues the one language of the Holy Spirit (Acts 2:1-4). This was a symbol of the greatest degree of God's Spirit poured out and the greatest approval of Heaven. Each given the same Spirit and heavenly grace, the apostles remained in the Spirit as one; nothing one had was his alone but belonged to all. Heavenly power was given to them, and God's favor and approval guided their lives. Seeking divine approval and grace from above, we too may pour our self out to God, shaking the very ground of Heaven; and our faith too may be established and unshaken. May we too be bold for Christ, seeking the unquenchable power of the Holy Spirit.

Chapter 3

Moving Forward for God

Tell the Israelites to go forward. But you lift up your staff, and stretch out your hand over the sea and divide it, that the Israelites may go into the sea on dry ground. — **Exodus 14:15-16**

In the Old Testament, God often fought against the enemy with raging winds, thus earning the deliverance for His people. After Israel's first deliverance, they seemed hedged in at all sides: in front, a raging sea, on either side, mountain peaks, and from behind, Pharaoh pursued them. Had they looked up, they would have seen a hurricane of winds raging. "The Lord drove the sea back by a strong east wind all night, and turned the sea into dry land; and the waters were divided" (vs. 21). Only when Israel was trapped did the triumph come; stormy winds held back the sea for them to cross. Israel was held not by the sea but by God's hands; the very waters they crossed shined the glory of His majesty and deliverance.

When the Egyptians attempted to follow the Israelites into the divided waters, God further commanded Moses to "stretch out your hand over the sea, so that the water may come back upon the Egyptians, upon their chariots and chariot drivers" (vs. 26). Then Moses, with all of Israel, sang to God: "You blew with your wind, the sea covered them; they sank like lead in the mighty waters" (Exodus 15:10).

After the deliverance and victory had come, we can never help but to lift our heart and sing joy to our Conqueror. When we turn from discouragement and lack of trust, the Holy Spirit awakens, and God will breathe His divine strength into our soul. Our soul, like a bird that flies beyond the clouds, must never lose its skyward look. We must keep hope; we must keep faith; we must keep courage. When our soul keeps its skyward look, we always will see God through the storms, the clouds, and the sunny days. We can never see the sun when we look to where it sets. If we look to the east, the sun rises; and even if there are clouds around it, the glory of God shines through.

'Put out into the deep water and let down your nets for a catch.' —
Luke 5:4

It is not surprising that Simon caught fish when he let down his net into deeper water. The fish do not thrive in the shallows near the shore. The depths of the water into which we sail depends on how completely we have cut off our ties to the shore: the greatness of our need and anxiety about the future.

Just as the fish were to be caught in the deep waters, so too are our needs met in the deep things of God. The Holy Spirit opens our eyes to see the crystal-clear meaning of God's deep waters when we sail deeper into them. The Holy Spirit is a sweet and tender guide, a thoughtful anticipator of our needs, and a supernatural sculptor of our circumstances. God has made all the vast depths fit together with each of our talents and desires.

Ezekiel describes the depths of the waters into which we are to sail: "The man measured one thousand cubits, and then led me through the water; and it was ankle-deep. Again, he measured one thousand, and led me through the water; and it was knee-deep. Again, he measured one thousand, and led me through the water; and it was up to the waist. Again, he measured one thousand, and it was a river that I could not cross, for the water had risen; it was deep enough to swim in, a river that could not be crossed" (Ezekiel 47:3-5). We must not be content to wade out into the water only to go ankle-deep, or knee-deep, or even waist-deep. Let us be submerged in the Holy Spirit and God's river of life. We must sail into the deep waters of God's great love, knowing that He who does the measuring will never let us drown.

> **Stand therefore, and fasten the belt of truth around your waist, and put on the breastplate of righteousness. As shoes for your feet put on whatever will make you ready to proclaim the gospel of peace. With all of these, take the shield of faith, with which you will be able to quench all the flaming arrows of the evil one. Take the helmet of salvation, and the sword of the Spirit, which is the word of God.** —Ephesians 6:14-17

Paul speaks not of our mortal enemies but spiritual ones. As stated earlier in the same chapter, "For our struggle is not against enemies of blood and flesh, but against the rulers, against the authorities, against the cosmic powers of this present darkness, against the spiritual forces of evil in the heavenly places" (vs. 12).

The need to take up the full armor of God is to fight against these enemies who assault us in the things that belong to our soul and labor to deface the heavenly image in our heart. We must stand as a soldier stands in battle, therefore, and resolve in God's grace not to yield to any attack by Satan. In what way are we to do this, and how are we to be armed? Paul proceeds to specify and in doing so describes the ancient armor of a soldier. With this armor -provided through the grace of our Leader- we are girded securely for battle. There is no putting off this armor until we have done our warfare and finished our course. Notice that Paul never names anything to protect the back of the warrior. There is no fit armor for the one who turns back or turns aside from their spiritual fight. The armor of God is the only fit protection to keep us safe in our fight. The only way for the warrior is forward.

Truth and sincerity are the girdle. Its importance lay in being first mentioned, and all of the other pieces of our armor are girded here. The righteousness of Christ imputed to us is a breastplate against the arrows of divine wrath. The righteousness of Christ implanted in us fortifies the heart against the attacks of Satan. Our resolution must be as armor to our legs, and to stand our ground or to march forward in rugged paths, the feet must be shod with the preparation of the Gospel of peace. Faith, as relying on unseen objects, receiving Christ and the benefits of redemption, and so deriving grace from Him is like a shield: a defense in every way. The devil is the wicked one. Powerful temptations, by which the soul is set on fire, are darts Satan shoots at us. Applying the Word of God and the grace of Christ quenches the darts of temptation. Salvation must be our helmet. A good hope of salvation -a Scriptural expectation of victory- will purify the soul and keep it from being defiled by Satan.

To the Christian armed for defense in battle, Paul recommends only one weapon of attack - the sword of the Spirit, which is the word of God- which is enough. It subdues and mortifies evil desires and blasphemous thoughts as they rise within, and answers unbelief and error as they assault from without. Prayer must fasten all the other parts of our Christian armor, and we must pray by the grace of God and the Holy Spirit, in dependence on, and according to His teaching. We must preserve in particular requests, notwithstanding discouragements. We must pray not for ourselves only but for all saints. Our enemies are mighty, and we are without strength; but our Redeemer is almighty, and in the power of His might, we will overcome.

The Lord said to Moses in Midian, 'Go back to Egypt; for all those who were seeking your life are dead.' So, Moses took his wife and his sons, put them on a donkey, and went back to the land of Egypt; and Moses carried the staff of God in his hand. —Exodus 4:19-20

Moses did not delay! After hearing what God had told him, and the signs performed (vs. 3-9), he readily took up his sons and wife and turned back to Egypt. As God commissioned Moses to go thither, so he did. Even though his fear and doubt were set before the Lord (vs. 10), God comforts him with His promises (vs. 10-12); so, He does likewise to each of His people who seek to hear His voice. We must have instant obedience. Delayed obedience is disobedience. When we do not like His answer or when there is a delay in His answer, it is tempting to ask God, "Why?" This hinders God's work in our lives and slows our progress to accomplish great things for Him. If Moses had disobeyed, the great story of the exodus would not have come to pass. Martin Luther once said, "A true believer will crucify the question 'why!' He will simply obey without questioning." Moses does not go alone. Not only is the Lord with him, but Moses takes the staff of God in his hand: "Your rod and your staff, they comfort me" (Psalm 23:4). This is our comfort, that God is with us.

> *Be ready in the morning, and come up in the morning to Mount Sinai and present yourself there to me, on the top of the mountain.*
> —Exodus 34:2

The dawn of each new day is the start of another day with our Lord: another day to listen, another day to act, and another day to trust His plans for us, walking with steady feet and a humbled heart the road He has for us to follow. What was not done yesterday may be accomplished today, and goals that were not met in the past may be reached this day. We mustn't let our past affect the present, but let our present change our future for God's glory! God does not look back; He looks forward, keeping His eyes focused toward His plans for us this day. We too must focus our attention on the day at hand. We cannot look back, grieving over past sorrows, fretting over unachieved goals, or worrying if we have pleased the Lord.

This is the day to please our Maker; this is the day to walk in faith with Him. "This is the day that the Lord has made; let us rejoice and be glad in it" (Psalm 118:24). Each day that dawns is a new day to live for His good pleasure. Yesterday is history, tomorrow is a mystery, but today is a gift; perhaps that is why it is called 'the present.' We are to receive the gift of each new day and live it to our fullest, walking in faith with the Lord. With this in mind, the American poet and philosopher, **Ralph Waldo Emmerson**, writes that *"With the past, I have nothing to do; nor with the future. I live now."*[2]

> *My servant Moses is dead. Now proceed to cross the Jordan, you and all this people, into the land that I am giving to them, to the Israelites.* —Joshua 1:2

---

[2] Harvard University (1969, pp. 241) *Journals and Miscellaneous Notebooks of Ralph Waldo Emmerson, VII: 1838-1842.*

As it says in God's Word, He did not hold back a time to let the Israelites weep for the death of their beloved Moses. Joshua was commissioned at that time to move forward with Israel and cross the Jordan River. Weeping by a grave will never bring back the treasure of a loved one, nor will any blessing come from it.

Sorrow casts deep scars that are written upon our heart. Yet, sorrow that is endured in the right spirit impacts our growth to move forward for God. Our truest richest comfort through sorrow is to pass on toward the goal. When we turn from past sorrows, walking out of the fog of cloudy days, we can better see the Lord's path which He means for us to continue to follow. The sun shines the brightest when we escape the clouds of sorrow and let Him guide us.

As we continue toward the goal God set before us -not hindered by sorrows, trials, or uncertainties- our Lord continues to give us His bountiful blessings. If Israel had stopped for a moment to grieve for the death of Moses, they would have put the Lord's interests at risk, and His plans for them to prosper would have been hindered. God promised Joshua and all of Israel to give them a bounty of blessings in the land of His promise; they had simply to move on to that goal. We move forward waiting, watching, and hoping. May we also believe that God leads us to the good of His everlasting blessings, just as David declared, 'I believe that I shall see the goodness of the Lord in the land of the living" (Psalm 27:13).

And I will turn all my mountains into a road, and my highways shall be raised up. —Isaiah 49:11

Though not always readily evident, there is always a path over the mountains. When we walk by faith, God's way -even through the mountains- must be our way; the faint track never dies out if our faith is meek and keen-sighted. There are difficulties in the way to Heaven, yet the grace of God will carry us over them and turn even the mountains into a path. This denotes the free invitations and the encouraging promises of the Gospel and the outpouring of the Spirit. When we come to the mountains, God will make a way over them! God makes even our obstacles to serve His purpose. These obstacles are needed to obtain a greater spiritual growth; they can become for us the very gifts from God that we have been praying for such as love, patience, and gentleness by enduring the very trials that develop these characteristics. God put the very mountains in our life; He can very easily level them.

Just as you do not know how the breath comes to the bones in the mother's womb, so you do not know the work of God, who makes everything. —Ecclesiastes 11:5

Simply put: questioning God is folly to us all, further hindering our faith-walk when we stumble over rocks, or come upon thorns, that to us seemed to have not been present. Although it is easy to question God when desires go amiss and unexplainable situations come upon us, we must remember that we do not fully understand why our Maker works in the ways that He does. Just as the works of many things of nature -not only the forming of a body in the mother's womb- cannot be explained, neither can the infinite God be fully explained. The plans He has, the desires He means to carry out, or the actions He takes in the world (let alone, in each of us, if we would but let Him work in our life). What we can and should do is to "cast our cares on Christ" (1 Peter 5:7) not only because He cares for us, but also because He is the author of days and the shaper of ways. Let us not question our Lord; may the doubts we have be replaced with strengthened faith, eventually leading us to trust our Maker.

I am confident of this, that the one who began a good work among you will bring it to completion by the day of Jesus Christ. —Philippians 1:6

Paul begins this verse with a statement of great confidence in the church at Philippi and hereafter all those who are children of Christ. While salvation from the penalty of sin happens at the moment a person accepts Christ, the process of becoming more like Christ is exactly that: a process. Paul is completely sure that this sanctification will continue in the lives of these believers, and all God's children. In particular, this assurance is grounded in the work of Jesus Christ. Paul has no doubt about their salvation and their faithful service to Christ. We too must have full confidence in this hope, in the promises of Scripture, and through the saving blood of Christ, knowing that the One who began a great restoration in us will finish His work until He sees nothing but Christ reflected in each of us.

Feed my sheep. —John 21:17

In response to Peter's threefold declaration of love for Christ, the Lord replies with the threefold command to "feed my sheep."

Each of us is like "a sheep without a shepherd" (Mark 6:34): poor, desperate, and suffering sheep. Without the seed of Christ's truth planted in our soul, we are lost to the actions, beliefs, and cares of the world. For this very reason, Jesus asked His followers to be a leader to His flock: to feed His sheep by none other than the gift of grace. The witnesses with Christ were to further become witnesses *for* Him, leading His flock, feeding them by the truth and knowledge outlined in His Holy Word, teaching them to walk humbly in the way of love and grace.

20

Following His crucifixion, death, and resurrection, the heart-searching and all-knowing God stresses the threefold question of love upon the apostle Peter, knowing that days earlier he was the one that denied Him three times. This puts Peter in a grievous state, knowing that he had denied his Lord, and yet, knowing the cost of true loyalty and love. There is no doubt that in his mind, Peter had -after three years of walking with the Lord- established the greatest degree of love for Christ, yet in his heart, he regrets loathsomely the act he of denying the Lord. Peter was to be the first appointed shepherd of God's flock, "an elder and witness of Christ's sufferings" (1 Peter 5:1). However, before he could serve God faithfully, his heart had to be tested. God puts our sincerity, loyalty, and love to the test. No one who does not love the Good Shepherd more than anything, anyone, or any title can be qualified to feed the flock of God's pasture. Each of Christ's children is to walk in His ways and practice His acts of love and grace, thus in one way or another, feeding God's flock of wandering sheep, earning the "crown of glory that will never fade away" (1 Peter 5:4) when the Chief Shepherd returns.

A great follower makes a great leader. —**Pastor Larry Marshall**

For to me, living is Christ and dying is gain. If I am to live in the flesh, that means fruitful labor for me; and I do not know which I prefer. I am hard-pressed between the two: my desire is to depart and be with Christ, for that is far better. — Philippians 1:21-23

Death is a great loss to a carnal, worldly man, for he loses all his earthly comforts and all his hopes. To a true believer, death is gain, for it is the end of all his weakness and misery. It delivers him from all the evils of life and brings him to possess the chief good: eternity with God. Paul's difficulty was not between living in this world and living in Heaven, but between serving Christ in this world and enjoying Him in another: not between two evil things was he ensnared, but between two good things.

See the power of faith and divine grace; it can make one willing to depart from this world to be with Christ. We are compassed with sin in this world; but when with Christ, we shall know no sin, temptation, sorrow, or death. Those who have the most reason to desire to depart should be willing to remain in the world as long as God has any work for them to do. The more Christ is reflected in one's life, the more fruitful service is done for Him. This is what Paul struggled against: the fruitful labor he had yet to do for Christ's name. He would remain in this world as long as God had service for him to offer and only later depart to be with Christ forever. This is the view of life and death that all true believers should have: to live is to serve Christ, and to die is gain: to be with Him forever.

21

This will give you an opportunity to testify. —Luke 21:13

We are given here an opportunity to be witnesses for Christ. Jesus warns that His disciples will be arrested. They will have an opportunity to display their testimony for Christ before kings and rulers, but they should not fear and should not practice what to say. Jesus says, "I will give you words" (vs. 15) and wisdom that will confound those who persecute the Lord's disciples. Similarly, through the grace of God and the baptism of His Holy Spirit, we are given that very opportunity: to keep the message of the Gospel heard and confirmed throughout a hurting world. Christ's children may leave their testimony, if not before kings, then before governments and rulers of today's world.

We come to Christ and are sent forth with a responsibility: to testify the truth to a world that has fallen to sin. Through what we have spiritually (and perhaps physically) experienced from our Maker, and the grace He's given us to stand by Christ's side, we are given both the opportunity and privilege to testify for His Kingdom, planting seeds in many lost souls, that they may be watered and nourished by the Holy Spirit, that Christ may begin to be seen in their life. Let us too by the grace of God and the guidance of the Holy Spirit testify for God's Kingdom and Christ's great love!

The passageway of the side chambers widened from story to story; for the structure was supplied with a stairway all around the temple. For this reason, the structure became wider from story to story. One ascended from the bottom story to the uppermost story by way of the middle one. —Ezekiel 41:7

God is building a temple within each of His children's souls; a place where His Holy Spirit can dwell. This temple dwindles, however, while we stay at the bottom when we should be ascending the stairs of our faith, moving always closer to Heaven, closer to God. We rest content at the bottom, knowing the stairs of life are hard to climb, too troubling and trying for our weak faith, too steep to see the summit, and too uncertain to spur us onward. Our focus need not be on the stairs of our life; rather, we need to focus on the One who waits for us at the summit. When we make Christ the creator and cornerstone of our life, we climb the stairs with confidence, turning aside from doubt, trembling, fear, and uncertainty. Leaving fear and doubt behind, we can further ascend upward where our soul may bask in the glory of God's kingdom. God is not content to build up our faith, only to let it sit beneath the clouds.

Too low they build who build beneath the stars; we must build beyond the stars! Let us take this temple of faith and build it upward, rising always to a higher level of belief, securing the foundation of each new level, that it may stand firm in Christ. It is only at the top of the temple that we can look down and see God's New Jerusalem, and it is only at the top that we can feel the fullness of God's glory shining upon us. Let us go forth with strength and confidence, living our best for God, reviving and replenishing our faith with the truth that the summit holds a much greater joy.

Beloved, I do not consider that I have made it my own; but this one thing I do: forgetting what lies behind and straining forward to what lies ahead, I press on toward the goal for the prize of the heavenly call of God in Christ Jesus. —Philippians 3:13-14

In the unity of this chapter, Paul speaks of two goals: one based on the law of the flesh, and one set on the progression of faith in Christ and the end goal it brings one to receive.

Many warnings Paul gives: these all pertain to the flesh, and the keeping of the law of this world; these in unison are "enemies of the cross of Christ" (vs. 18). But the ones crucified with Christ, those circumcised into the true calling of faith, press onward, seeking the heavenly calling in which we are invited to partake, calling ourselves no longer slaves to sin but "citizens of heaven" (vs. 20). So, this Paul does -forgetting the things of this world of sin, crucifying the love of the law, and focusing no longer on the things of the flesh- he focuses solely on the end goal to which his faith will bring him: eternal life in the heavenly realm with his Savior. Brothers and sisters, may we also follow this lead of leaving behind the things of this world. Let us move forward with a happy heart, seeking only Christ and our heavenly home.

John performed no sign, but everything that John said about this man was true. —John 10:41

John the Baptist never performed a miraculous sign that was physically noteworthy, but what he did touched the heart of God. He was a voice for Christ crying out "In the wilderness prepare the way of the Lord, make straight in the desert a highway for our God" (Isaiah 40:3). John was simply a witness to the Light. He was not a voice seen but rather heard. When common people looked at John the Baptist, they did not see him, they saw Christ. The world looks at the outside; God looks at the heart within, working to plant seeds to be sown for Christ. We are not to count ourselves worth little if all we perform on this earth is being a voice for the Lord; His light shines all the brighter when His beloved are witnesses for Him. Jesus Himself admits, "There is no one greater" (Luke 7:28). God sees the work within the simplest and meager of tasks.

23

> *Whatever your task, put yourselves into it, as done for the Lord and not for your masters.* —Colossians 3:23

Know that Christ is our Master. We must do our work heartily, not by mere force and necessity, grudgingly, and with murmurings, but from the heart and with goodwill, having true affection for our Master, knowing that the one we truly serve is God. Paul's words remind us that, regardless of our station in life, God is the one ultimately judging all we do, so all of our service is really for Him. From the lowliest of slaves to the greatly praised leader, every person is called to work for God's honor. We do not work for men or simply earthly goals, but to glorify our heavenly Father and Master. Living for the Lord's honor is relevant in all of our work contexts.

> *Finally, beloved, whatever is true, whatever is honorable, whatever is just, whatever is pure, whatever is pleasing, whatever is commendable, if there is any excellence and if there is anything worthy of praise, think about these things.*

> *Keep on doing the things that you have learned and received and heard and seen in me, and the God of peace will be with you.* —Philippians 4:8-9

-And-

> *By contrast, the fruit of the Spirit is love, joy, peace, patience, kindness, generosity, faithfulness, gentleness, and self-control. There is no law against such things.* —Galatians 5:22-23

Paul gives a perfect example of these spiritual fruits, and how we are to live out each one, desiring to act upon those things which bring God glory and are pleasing to Him: namely, thoughts and acts wrought in the soul; these are areas of importance in the life of the believer. Some of these fruits bloom only in the canyon (the hard times): patience, kindness, faithfulness, and gentleness. The fruits that bloom in the canyons are more beautiful than the fruit that grow in the open prairie (the easy times). The Master can find the blooms in us, even where there are jagged rocks.

The canyons we experience are for our own good (Hebrews 12:10). It should be our care to act under the guidance and power of the Holy Spirit. Those who desire to give themselves up to the leading of the Holy Spirit are not under the law of the flesh as a covenant works, but they desire for holiness and show that they have a part in the salvation of the Gospel. Obtaining the fruits of the Spirit plainly shows that one is led by the Spirit, not by the flesh. Believers are commanded to live according to God's ways. He does the work yet gives us work to do. Believers are called to trust in the Lord, and to serve the Lord. Paul set an example for how to do both. He was faithful in prayer yet gave every bit of his life to serve the Lord. The apostle sets the example: his doctrine and life are bound in unison; he practiced what he preached. The example Paul sets is one to be practiced in the life of each believer. By bringing forth these spiritual fruits, we are brought closer to God, basking in His peace. And whether our praise comes from man or no, it will come from the Lord.

Yet you do not even know what tomorrow will bring. What is your life? For you are a mist that appears for a little while and then vanishes. — James 4:14

James asks his readers to consider the temporary and fragile state of our own life: merely being a mist in the wind; soon to return to dust as we were (Genesis 3:19). We must recognize the arrogance of thinking we are masters of our own fate; in contrast, we cannot predict or control what happens in the morrow. How vain it is to look for anything good without God's blessing and guidance! We are to carry with us an awareness that our every moment is dependent on God's grace, mercy, and will. Let us plan for future good, but let us do so with the guidance of God's presence which He gives us through the Holy Spirit.

For you were called to freedom, brothers and sisters; only do not use your freedom as an opportunity for self-indulgence, but through love become slaves to one another. For the whole law is summed up in a single commandment, 'You shall love your neighbor as yourself.' — Galatians 5:13-14

We are not to use our freedom in Christ as a free ticket to please ourselves; but being led by the Spirit, we are to walk in the Spirit which is solely in love. Happy are those who serve one another: weeping with those who weep, rejoicing with those who rejoice, setting the example of the Gospel call. In such a way, we shall show the very love that Paul urges us to embrace, not just toward our brothers and sisters but to each of our neighbors, looking on them as Christ looks on them: with unquenchable love and ceaseless grace, perhaps in turn planting a seed for Christ. Paul reminds us of the power of love: "A little yeast leavens the whole batch of dough." A little bit of love spreads Christ's love amidst a hurting world.

For we have become partners of Christ, if only we hold our first confidence firm to the end. —Hebrews 3:14

The greatest challenge in receiving great blessings from God is holding on until the end, but this is the road of Christ's child. Permanence is the quality of the true believer. This is proof that we are saved. This is not easy, but God gives us strength. When we hold to the truth of Christ, we are like a tree planted firmly in the ground, not swayed by the wind or beaten down by sudden showers. The confidence in Christ that our Heavenly Father gave us at the start must remain as light always guiding our way. When we keep the light of Christ always with us, our faith will not be trampled by the darkness of Hell. Let us run the race "in such a way that you may win it" (1 Corinthians 9:24). May we not only run to touch the finish line but to pass over it.

So that you may not become sluggish, but imitators of those who through faith and patience inherit the promises. —Hebrews 6:12

The Biblical heroes do not only call to us the necessity of faith and the heights of the summit to which their faith has reached, but also remind us of the patience required for this faith to be carried out and perfected. We mustn't remove ourselves from the hands of God or miss His lessons of loving discipline due to lively fears, doubts, or   discouragements. The Father tests His saints by fire, water, and the heavy blow of His heavenly hammer. Just as steel is refined by fire and shaped with the hammer, so also, God shapes His saints to bear the perfect reflection of His Son. Many cannot withstand this process; when the first or second or even third blow hits, our grasp is loosened from the Mighty Forger. Instead of keeping our eyes fixed on the One who holds the hammer, we tend to turn aside, fearing the mighty fires of doubt and the heavy hammer blows of woe. If we cannot withstand His tempering process, we will be thrown onto the scrap heap of unforged souls. Be of good cheer, He gives us the needed strength.

Like the Biblical heroes, martyrs, and saints, we need to hold firm to the grasp of God, and His promised rewards. We must stand still when the fires of life are the hottest, exercising faith and patience; later we will become "a harvest of blessing" (Hebrews 12:11). God's saints are defined by their suffering. When we have waited patiently through our trials and faithfully endured the blows of the hammer, our life will be as polished gold in the hands of our God.

Chapter 4

God's Way and God's Timing

Then Moses turned again to the Lord and said, 'O Lord, why have you mistreated this people? Why did you ever send me?'
— Exodus 5:22

One of my favorite stories in the Old Testament is the story of Moses leading the Israelites out of captivity into the Promise Land. Although Moses could have been Pharaoh, taking his seat as the most powerful man in the world at that time, God called him to another mission. Moses chose to follow God's calling and not his own. This was the much harder, crucial, and devastating path; but through the devastations, hardships, and doubts, God carried out His promise to lead Israel to freedom. God never promised to Moses, and He never promised to us, that the road He chooses would be smooth and steady. He did promise, as He does countless times in His Word, that He will be with us always. Many times Moses cries out to God, "Why do bad things keep happening? Why did you send me to lead these people? Why has Israel turned away from you and chosen their own path?" God was not content to answer such questions. He was content simply to continue to stay faithful in His words and guidance to Moses and all of Israel.

If God always allowed us smooth sailing, He could not show us His majesty, His faithfulness, and His grace. If there was no wave on the seas of life, God could not reach down and calm the waters; He could not offer His hands for us to grasp. Lessons are learned, and greater wisdom is gathered to those who seek after the ways of the Lord, following His calling as opposed to their own. Is it not true that Moses was named one of the greatest prophets of God?

When the soles of the feet of the priests who bear the ark of the Lord, the Lord of all the earth, rest in the waters of the Jordan, the waters of the Jordan flowing from above shall be cut off.
—Joshua 3:13

We need to learn to take God at His word, walking straight ahead in obedience even when we see no way to move forward. Often, we are sidetracked by difficulties because we expect our barriers to be removed before we come

27

to them or pass through them; we stand still, waiting for obstacles to be removed from our path. We need only to follow the Lord's leading, moving straight ahead in faith, as if there were no obstacles at all. God's plan for Israel was to move straight into the Jordan River. When they listened to the Lord, the waters were cut off as soon as they set foot in them. When our faithfulness prevails, God's plan is freely revealed. When our faithfulness honors the Lord, He, in turn, will honor that faithfulness. As Paul reminds us in his second letter to the Corinthians, "For we walk by faith, not by sight" (2 Corinthians 5:7). We need not focus on the barriers around us but only on the Holy Spirit's voice that whispers in our heart the will of our Lord.

> *But the hill country shall be yours, for though it is a forest, you shall clear it and possess it to its farthest borders.* —Joshua 17:18

Joshua tells these two tribes that what was fallen to their share would be a sufficient lot for them if they would but work and fight for it. Should they desire a larger share of land, *they* would have to work to obtain it. Some people would at all cost excuse themselves from work. Nothing serves this purpose better than having rich and powerful relations, able to provide for them, making them prone to desire partial and unfaithful disposal of what is entrusted to others. This is what the tribe of Joseph strived to do: use the Canaanites as an excuse for their lack of effort to move forward and work for their share of land. Instead of turning to God for help, they looked to their neighbors, desiring from them an equal share of land. But there is more real kindness in pointing out the advantages within reach, and in encouraging men to make the best of them, than in granting indulgences to sluggishness and sloth.

Idleness magnifies every difficulty and danger; this is especially the case in our spiritual work and warfare. Without God, we can do nothing and are prone to sit still and attempt nothing. If we belong to Him, He will stir us up to our best endeavors and teach us to come to Him for help; then our lands will be enlarged and complaining silenced, or rather, turned into joyful thanksgiving. Difficulties are sent to reveal what God can and will do in answer to a faith that prays and acts. Did Joshua not promise the tribe of Joseph that they would drive out the Canaanites if they but attempted to fight?

> *He restores my soul.* —Psalm 23:3

The Lord restores our soul from its errors of wandering. No creature is more ready to go astray and more at a loss to find its way back than a sheep. All of us, like sheep, have gone astray and are still too prone to do so, to leave the right way of truth and duty and follow a bypath. But when God shows us our errors, allows us repentance, and brings us back to our duty. He restores our soul; and if He did not do this, we would wander endlessly and be undone. With joy, David reflects that he has a shepherd and that shepherd is Jehovah. A flock of sheep, gentle and harmless, feeding in flourishing pastures under the care of a skillful, watchful, and loving shepherd reflects the flock of believers brought back to the Shepherd of their soul. The greatest abundance is but a dry pasture to a wicked man who relishes in it only for the pleasures of the body; but to a godly man, who by faith tastes the goodness of God in all his enjoyments, it is a green pasture flowering with God's blessings. We are blessed with the green pastures. Let us not think it enough to pass through them, but let us abide in them with our Good Shephard leading us.

> **When you pass through the waters, I will be with you; and through the rivers, they shall not overwhelm you; when you walk through fire you shall not be burned, and the flame shall not consume you.**
> —Isaiah 43:2

God never opens paths until we come to them, or removes obstacles until they stand in our way. Too often we look many miles ahead, waiting for God to pave the way for tomorrow; we stand still; we make no progress today. We must be *in* the floodwaters before we can claim God's promise to rebuke the storm, and the giants must be *in front of us* before God can send His army of angels to fight for us. Only when we fall can God pick us up. Step by step God leads us along the path He has chosen for us and provides us with the strength to walk the portion chosen for today. We are given living grace for each new day. Waiting for tomorrow's sun to shine, doubt darkens our eyes from the light that shines today.

> **A time to tear, and a time to sew; a time to keep silence, and a time to speak.** —Ecclesiastes 3:7

-And-

> **I know that whatever God does endures forever; nothing can be added to it, nor anything taken from it; God has done this, so that all should stand in awe before him. That which is, already has been; that which is to be, already is; and God seeks out what has gone by.**
> —Ecclesiastes 3:14-15

Change allows us to adapt to new situations and to further grow inside. To expect unchanging happiness in a changing world will always end in disappointment; but while the circumstances of this life change, God does not (Hebrews 13:8). Even in the midst of a changing world, His promises remain; His purposes are always steadfast; and His timing is set perfectly, further allowing His Children to accomplish great things in His Son's name. We must accept each day as a gift from God's hands; He has a reason and a time for all things under Heaven (Ecclesiastes 3:1). We may be ignorant of His timing, but we are called to enjoy life in the present and trust in His sovereignty. Despite the change in this world, we are still called to be His witnesses, making disciples for Christ (Matthew 28:19). Pastor Larry Marshall once in his teachings asserted that, *Life can be a mystery, but we can trust fully in His wisdom and grace.*

> **When clouds are full,**
> **they empty rain on the earth;**
> **whether a tree falls to the south or to the north,**
> **in the place where the tree falls,**
> **there it will lie.**
> **Whoever observes the wind will not sow;**
> **and whoever regards the clouds will not reap.** - Ecclesiastes 11:3-4

In conclusion to verse 2, Solomon points out that not everything is in our control. Many things are uncertain: just as a cloud fills with rain, emptying it upon the earth, or a tree that falls to the ground remains in the place it falls. Considering each act of God and analyzing possible outcomes, a child of God falls short of their duty, failing to bring further glory to God. May we not look for rain clouds but seek God's showers of blessings. Let us not consider the way of the wind but rather listen for God's voice in its midst. Fear not the inconveniences of life, but do the duty given to you, with full regard to the promises, provisions, and power of God. It is wisdom to accept events -be they good or ill- as they occur, knowing that each act of God is divinely designed.

> **But all of you are kindlers of fire, lighters of firebrands. Walk in the flame of your fire, and among the brands that you have kindled! This is what you shall have from my hand: you shall lie down in torment.** —Isaiah 50:11

The prophet proclaims a crucial warning to all those who walk in darkness and try to help themselves find the light: those "who carry out a plan, but not mine; who make an alliance, but against my will, adding sin to sin" (Isaiah 30:1). When we are in the darkness, it is tempting to try and find our own way out instead of trusting the Lord and relying on Him. We reason out our own conclusions and accept paths that are not in line with God's will. These are the fires of our own kindling.

When we look up to the beacon of light we have set ablaze, the light shines but not toward heaven; we look up to the thorns on the mountainside where our beacon rests. Faithful brothers and sisters, we must never try to get out of a dark place but in God's timing and by His way. The darkened paths of life are set before us, that from our Great Teacher, we may learn lessons that are desperately needed: lessons of patience, lessons of trust, lessons of faith, and lessons of grace. Premature deliverance always bypasses God's work in our life. We needn't try and find our own way out of the darkness, but we should be rest assured knowing that the Lord is always present. He never promised a clear, lightened road, so we mustn't take Him for a liar or deceiver. When we leave everything to Him without exception, we can faithfully say, "Not what I want, but what you want" (Mark 14:36).

Life is always better when we're in the center of God's will! — **Kelby Klassen**

I will lead on slowly, according to the pace of the cattle that are before me and according to the pace of the children. —Genesis 33:14

Our Lord never leads His children beyond what we can bear or makes us take another step beyond what we can endure. If we cannot go forward, we needn't despair; God will either give us the strength to move on or call a sudden halt so that we may rest.

May Jacob's care and tender affection to his family and flocks remind us of the Good Shepherd of our soul, for "he will gather the lambs in his arms, and carry them in his bosom, and gently lead the mother sheep" (Isaiah 40:11).

But Moses said to the people, 'Do not be afraid, stand firm, and see the deliverance that the Lord will accomplish for you today; for the Egyptians whom you see today you shall never see again.'—Exodus 14:13

There was no way open to Israel but upward, and thence their deliverance came. We may be in the way of duty, following God, and hastening toward Heaven, yet may be troubled on every side. Our deliverance is only in the Lord. Like the Israelites, we can find ourselves in straits, that He may bring us to our knees before Him. Some cried out against Moses; fear set them murmuring as if God was not still able to work miracles. They quarreled with Moses for bringing them out of Egypt and were angry with God for the greatest kindness ever done for them. Moses encouraged the people not to be afraid. It is always our duty and interest when we cannot get out of troubles, to get above our fears; let them quicken our prayers and petitions but not silence our faith and hope. Stand still, do not think of how to save yourself either by fighting or flying; wait for God's orders and observe them. Compose yourself -by confidence in God- into peaceful thoughts of the great

31

salvation God is about to work for you. If God brings His people into straits, He will certainly bring them out in His good time.

Be still before the Lord, and wait patiently for him. —Psalm 37:7

What a difficult thing it is to be still and wait! Perhaps we make this task so difficult because we wait in the wrong way and at the wrong place, aimlessly pondering over the question 'what if', and selfishly wondering if our desires will ever be carried out, or despairing over the worst possible outcomes. This type of patience -pushing our Maker to get the work done- never allows Him to finish it. We are simply driven to madness in the attempt, and we fail to honor Him. We rather need to wait where the Lord can meet us and the Holy Spirit can reflect blessings of the Father's love on us. When we wait in this way, worry is eliminated. We can hold on to His promise that He will come to us in due time. Self-works are eliminated through patience. Our work should be according to God's plan. Through this patient believing, we are shown greater glory. Patience eliminates weakness. We no longer have to view the time as wasted; it is a time that God is preparing the resources for us to receive His even greater blessings and accomplish even greater things for Him, even if it is just a little accomplishment in our eyes. Our time to ponder becomes time to pray. The selfishness of our wondering becomes time to worship. And the time of despair becomes the time to remember His goodwill. We must stand firm in our faith: allowing it to become so strong that in times of doubt, we can put our heart to rest, trusting God. Living stillness is born of this trust.

We know that all things work together for good for those who love God, who are called according to his purpose. —Romans 8:28

Paul states clearly in verse 29 what that purpose is: if we are God's without reserve, we know that He always works for our good. But how many of us can hold to that truth, especially in trying times? All things in His children's lives -be it favorable or not- God uses as scattered materials, fitting it all together to work perfectly for our good and the accomplishment of His divine purpose. Being a witness to this truth, the disciple answers his own question and declares a fundamental truth for the Christian: If He is for us, **no one** can be against us (Vs. 31). Each one has been called; but to follow the Gospel call of Christ is to be born again in Christ, to be one with God, thus having the favor of the Father and He working for our good, so that we may carry out His purpose to reflect His likeness.

But those who wait for the Lord shall renew their strength, they shall mount up with wings like eagles, they shall run and not be weary, they shall walk and not faint. —Isaiah 40:31

The prophet ought to have said, 'Those who *serve* the Lord will have an *imperishable* strength.' To wait on the Lord is to serve Him, learning His desires and direction for us and acting on them. This will bring to our minds the knowledge and reverence of God. He asks us to serve Him faithfully, continually leaning on and trusting Him until we have come to the end of our faith, which is the salvation of our soul. Strength comes by obeying the Lord, acting on His commands, and trusting His leadership. Only then will our physical and spiritual strength rise toward God, higher than any eagle dares to soar. If we go forth in our own strength, we shall faint and utterly fail; but having our heart and our hopes in Heaven, we shall be carried above all difficulties and be enabled to lay hold of the prize of our high calling in Christ Jesus.

For surely I know the plans I have for you, says the Lord, plans for your welfare and not for harm, to give you a future with hope. — Jeremiah 29:11

-And-

He has made everything suitable for its time. —Ecclesiastes 3:11

I lean on this truth often, more so when my plans fail and I don't have another place to turn. I feel foolish, not being patient and listening to His voice calling me. But then I smile, hearing His voice in my ear, telling me that He has better plans, and redirects the broken and torn road I've tried to travel without Him. We often strive to follow what seems to be the smooth trail; the unhindered path that appears so likely to lead to a secure destination. Trying to see the end of the road and its fulfillment, we go forward, never once acknowledging our Heavenly Father or asking which way He means for us to walk, or waiting on His timing for us to walk the road He has laid. Many times, this verse from God's prophet comes to me as a source of redemption, refreshment, and calm. Often our plans fail, and the roads we follow without God's guidance end at the wrong destination. But then God smiles from Heaven, reminding His children: "I know the plans to lead you; and my guidance will not fail you." Our Father will often let us go forward with our own plans, not because He desires to see us falter, but because He loves us so dearly and means to teach us the truth of this verse. The more we stumble upon our own road, the more we look up to God. When we continue to look up, God continues to strengthen our faith. With stronger faith comes stronger means to trust God, knowing that His plans always lead us to a firm foundation. So, let us not only read this verse, but live it, knowing that God's plans never have and never will fail us.

The Lord is not slow about his promise, as some think of slowness, but is patient with you, not wanting any to perish, but all to come to repentance. —2 Peter 3:9

At the time Peter wrote his letter, many people were anticipating the second coming of Christ. Peter reminds his readers that God's timing does not run on a human schedule, to God "one day is like a thousand years, and a thousand years are like one day" (vs. 8). The Lord is not bound by the timing of humanity. Had the coming of Christ been sooner, God's desire to have more sons and daughters, more souls come to repentance would have been thwarted. God desires a large family: many sons and daughters come together in His Son's name. The more time given -as humanity measures time- the more time allowed for more people to come to repentance, if nothing else but by the power, guidance, and grace of the Spirit. We must "regard the patience of the Lord as salvation" (vs. 15) to His people. By His love and grace, more time is offered for more souls to come to Christ.

I consider that the sufferings of this present time are not worth comparing with the glory about to be revealed to us. —Romans 8:18

O how much the perfection hereafter surpasses the joys of this world! As indicated in Hebrews, we must suffer with Christ if we are to partake in His glory: "For they disciplined us for a short time as seemed best to them, but he disciplines us for our good, in order that we may share his holiness" (12:10). The sufferings of Christ's saints seem but a short while compared to the joy that awaits us. We are brought into a state of safety in hope of eternity; from this hope, we cannot find satisfaction in anything of time or sense. Earth's best cannot compare with Heaven's least, the finite cannot be compared to the infinite, and the carnal desires cannot be compared with the spiritual longings. These are but the sufferings of this *present time*; the world is not always to continue as it is; indeed, the whole creation seems to wait with earnest expectation for the period when the children of God shall be manifested in the glory prepared for them. We must have patience; Christ will come for His beloved, though to us He seems to tarry.

34

Chapter 5

God's Overflowing Blessings

Then go in, and shut the door behind you and your children, and start pouring into all these vessels; when each is full, set it aside. —
2 Kings 4:4

God will close us off to something divine, just as He closed the doors behind the widow and her sons. They were left alone, but it was in this inner quiet that God worked this divine miracle. The one pot of oil the woman had was always flowing, yet always full, filling countless vessels with oil. The springs that supported it are the very springs of "living water" (John 4:10) that support us, if only we too will take what we have and pour it out to the Lord. Our need is supported by God's blessings; He works with what we have, not with what we are waiting to receive from Him. God reveals Himself as the greatest in the most trying of circumstances. It was at the wedding in Cana that Jesus turned the water to wine (John 2:7-9), and while blocked by the Red Sea, the Lord parted it before the Israelites (Exodus 14:15-16). There was also the amazing miracle that king Nebuchadnezzar witnessed and came to believe in the one true God (Daniel 3:28-29). We must learn to lean on Him alone; He will enrich us with blessings both for this life and the next.

'Take the arrows'; and he took them. He said to the king of Israel, 'Strike the ground with them'; he struck three times, and stopped. Then the man of God was angry with him, and said, 'You should have struck five or six times; then you would have struck down Aram until you had made an end of it, but now you will strike down Aram only three times.' —2 Kings 13:18-19

It is a grief to God when we rely solely on our own strength, failing to cast our attention beyond the sight of our own physical strength.

Elisha assured the king of his success, if only he would have sought the help of God, not casting his cares to the powers of his own hands. To the dismay of the dying prophet, the king struck but only three times, as to the measure of his own strength. Had he looked up, seeking the power of God, he could have struck down deeper, harder, and firmer; thus, he would have gained that which was signified to him, the defeat of the Arameans. Listen,

O man, to the voice of God that speaks, if but by the power of the Spirit. He is waiting to come to our aid if we would but seek Him. It is wisdom to grasp the Divine Power of God, relying not merely on our own strengths. With this Divine Power, victory is assured.

> *For his anger is but for a moment; his favor is for a lifetime. Weeping may linger for the night, but joy comes with the morning.* — Psalm 30:5

It seems that God is angry when He turns His face from our sins. A holy, pure, and sinless God has but two ways to take the sins of humanity: to look on us with wrath and vengeance, or to turn His face from our sin. Because of the scar of sin left upon Christ, through Him, we find everlasting favor with God. He chooses, rather, to hide His face from the sinfulness of humanity; this seems to us as anger kindled in His heart when He turns away from us. The momentary affliction we receive from His Fatherly hand is but temporary and short-lived. When His hand is removed and He looks upon us once more, eternal grace and love are bound up in His divine favor. If we have the Lord's favor, we have eternal joy and happiness. God's anger will always turn into His favor. Moments of temporary abandonment will always be transformed into a lifetime of grace: this grace and favor lasts for all eternity. His mercies are always "new every morning" (Lamentations 3:23).

> *For a brief moment I abandoned you,*
> *but with great compassion I will gather you.*
> *In overflowing wrath for a moment*
> *I hid my face from you,*
> *but with everlasting love I will have compassion on you,*
> *says the Lord, your Redeemer.* —Isaiah 54:7-8

> *Taking the five loaves and the two fish, he looked up to heaven, and blessed and broke the loaves, and gave them to the disciples, and the disciples gave them to the crowds. And all ate and were filled; and they took up what was leftover of the broken pieces, twelve baskets full.* —Matthew 14:19-20

See in this miracle an emblem of the bread of life, which came down from Heaven to sustain our perishing soul. The provisions of Christ's Gospel appear mean and scanty to the world, yet they satisfy all that feed on the blessings of Christ in their heart by faith with thanksgiving. Notice that each time Jesus was asked to perform a great act, He first looked to Heaven and thanked the Father! Thanksgiving is always followed by the Father's blessings, however big or small those blessings may be. And even with very little,

God gives us enough to satisfy. May we always look to Him, thanking Him for the blessings of Heaven that satisfy our hungry soul.

> *'Give your servant therefore an understanding mind to govern your people, able to discern between good and evil; for who can govern this your great people?' It pleased the Lord that Solomon had asked this. God said to him, 'Because you have asked this, and have not asked for yourself long life or riches, or for the life of your enemies, but have asked for yourself understanding to discern what is right, I now do according to your word. Indeed, I give you a wise and discerning mind; no one like you has been before you and no one like you shall arise after you.'* — 1 Kings 3:9-12

The wiser and more considerate we are, the better acquainted we are with our own weaknesses. Solomon asked God to give him wisdom. We must pray for it, that it may help us in our particular calling. Being king, Solomon had a duty to fulfill, to govern his people rightly and justly. Praying for wisdom, Solomon could greatly govern such a people in causes and circumstances. Wisdom in Scripture is seen as good understanding. We are told that "wisdom gives life to the one who possesses it" (Ecclesiastes 7:12). On the contrary, "fools despise wisdom and instruction" (Proverbs 1:7). Those are accepted of God who prefer spiritual blessings to earthly good. It was a prevailing prayer, and prevailed for more than Solomon asked. God gave him wisdom, such as no other was ever blessed with, and in addition, God again gave Solomon riches and honor. If we seek after wisdom and grace, these will bring outward prosperity with them or sweeten the want of it. "If any of you is lacking in wisdom, ask God, who gives to all generously and ungrudgingly, and it will be given you" (James 1:5)

> *Every place that the sole of your foot will tread upon I have given to you, as I promised.* — Joshua 1:3

Much of the land of God's promises lays open before us, unclaimed and untrodden ground; it is in His goodwill that we possess it all. The land of God's promises is a magnificent territory for our faith to thrive; we have yet to walk it all. We are to march across the land of God's promises with obedience, measuring the length with the feet of faith. Sadly, like the Israelites, our faith goes only as far as our sight; thus, we occupy only a small percentage of the land. We must claim our total inheritance from our Father in the name of Christ. We must also lift our eyes to look north, south, east, and west, falling flat on the ground of *all* God's great promises. The land of the Lord's promise is too far for our eyes to see; thus, we need to keep walking the land, obtaining more of His promises each day through strengthened faith.

But he said to me, 'My grace is sufficient for you, for power is made perfect in weakness.' So, I will boast all the more gladly of my weakness, so that the power of Christ may dwell in me.
— 2 Corinthians 12:9

Many times in the Bible God's grace is bestowed to His children. The flames of the fiery furnace never scorched Shadrach, Meshach, or Abednego; their feet simply walked on the cooling waters of God's river of mercy (Daniel 3). How could David have written such beautiful psalms, many in the midst of sorrows? David saw his joys and his sorrows as a means to please God; he joyed in writing about them (Psalms of David). When the Ethiopians came up against Asa in massive numbers, he saw God, not fear, standing between him and his enemies (2 Chronicles 14).

Paul was thrown into prison more than once (Acts 16, Acts 24), yet many of his most beautiful letters proclaiming God's love and grace were written in dark prison cells. The Holy Spirit gave him light in those dark places. Moses led Israel out of its bondage in Egypt, across the Red Sea, and through many trials, yet they still sang hymns of praise to the Lord (Exodus 15). Knowing that God brought His people that far, Moses knew that no length was too far for God's mercies to stretch. Alone in the wilderness, our Lord was tempted by Satan (Matthew 4). Jesus overcame the temptation by looking for God's rivers of love and grace to quench His thirst. There are countless other examples of God giving His unending grace to His children. The Holy Spirit comes to us in the midst of hard times, trials, and persecutions bringing peace to our heart, rest to our mind, and hope to our soul. God's grace shines the brightest in the darkness; those who long to see it experience a glimpse of Heaven. A little bit of faith will bring our soul to Heaven, but great faith will bring Heaven to our soul. When we exercise great faith, we draw heavily upon God's great resources. We must fall flat on the ground of His grace; then when life does cause us to stumble, we will fall flat into the arms of His love.

Chapter 6

A Sure Foundation

Jesus Christ is the same yesterday and today and forever.
— Hebrews 13:8

Jesus Christ -the second person of the holy Godhead—shares in unison with the Father and Holy Spirit the divine nature of being omnipresent, omniscient, omnipotent, and omniferous: the unchangeable, almighty God. This fact of Christ being always who He was, is, and promises to be, encourages the believer to stand firm in the faith, knowing that promises made are promises kept. If our God was mutual and changeable, the believer would not know what to expect of Him. His promises would be procrastinations, His will would be unsettled, and His presence would be unsure and irregular.

Our Lord never changes even when our life does. We can rest assured that Christ is our rock, our one foundation on which our soul can rest secure. Christ's presence is one that remains with us through the gift of His Holy Spirit. When the going gets rough, He is the one with the unfailing plan to get us back on the right road once more. His promises made to us are promises kept, not delayed or wavering, but always in His perfect timing. And His strength is the unmatchable, unchangeable almighty power: when we are weak, He is strong. Brothers and sisters, may we rest assured knowing that we serve the all-faithful, all-powerful, never-changing Lord who is with His children always. In chapter one of Hebrews, the Christian finds a declaration of God's enduring nature:

In the beginning, Lord, you founded the earth,
and the heavens are the works of your hands;
they will perish, but you remain;
they will all wear out like clothing;
like a cloak you will roll them up,
and like clothing they will be changed.
But you are the same,
and your years will never end. —Hebrews 1:10-12

The Lord is my rock, my fortress, and my deliverer; my God, my rock in whom I take refuge, my shield, and the horn of my salvation, my stronghold. —Psalm 18:2

David often describes God as the one rock; this rock that David speaks of is more like to a boulder: unshakable, unmovable, and unbreakable. The one fortress on which we can rest securely. God has a very dependable and faithful character; He is the one in whom we can find shelter from our foes and stand strong upon when the whole world seems to triumph over us. Our safety and security are owed solely to God. A rock promises a firm foundation, one on which our faith can and will stand strong; He is the "chief cornerstone" (Psalm 118:22) of all we are in Christ Jesus. We can't forget the shield and horn He gives to us: the weapons that bring about our salvation and deliverance from our enemies. The shield protects and defends, holding back the fiery darts of darkness and doubt. A similar picture of God as a stronghold and a place of safe shelter can be found in the book of Proverbs: "The name of the Lord is a strong tower; the righteous run into it and are safe" (Proverbs 18:10). Those that truly love God may triumph in Him as their rock and refuge and may with confidence call upon Him.

My soul thirsts for God, for the living God. —Psalm 42:2

Our soul is thirsty. Many try to satisfy this thirst by setting their soul on perishing foundations: riches, possession, power, and the like. Such foundations are not firm; they soon break away and fall, supporting nothing. This is a temporary foundation, one set on the carnal desires - things that are seen of this world. A thirsty soul will never be fully satisfied on a foundation such as this. Our soul thirsts for the living God, "the chief cornerstone" (Psalm 118:22), the only firm foundation on which we can rest it; it fails to rest securely on anything short of the living God. Christ's love, mercy, grace, and strength are enough to sustain and satisfy the thirst and longing of our weary soul. Coming into the courtroom of Christ and communing with Him there, our soul drinks freely of the "living water" (John 4:10) and is satisfied forever, even if the entire world and all in it fall to ruin.

Jesus said to her, 'Everyone who drinks of this water will be thirsty again, but those who drink of the water that I will give them will never be thirsty. The water that I will give will become in them a spring of water gushing up to eternal life.' —John 4:13-14

The Living Water is the gift of the Spirit, planted firmly into the soul of the believer, always springing up like a fountain, heavenward, toward eternal life. The graces of the Spirit and His comforts satisfy the thirsting soul. The water of Jacob's well yielded a very short satisfaction. From whatever waters of comfort we drink, we shall thirst again. But whoever partakes of the Spirit of grace and the comforts of the Gospel shall never long for that which cannot satisfy the soul. And so, the promise is that they who believe in Christ and rest upon His love shall receive into their spirit new life, which shall rise in their heart like a fountain 'springing up into everlasting life.'

> *O Daniel, servant of the living God, has your God whom you faithfully serve been able to deliver you from the lions?* —Daniel 6:20

We need to remember that we serve the *living* God; we serve the very same living God today that thousands of years ago freed Daniel from the mouths of lions, parted the Red Sea that His people could cross over, and who, through loving grace, came down to be one amongst us, showing us a new way. There's a small part of a song I like to sing to myself. I have since forgotten most of the lyrics, but the message is the same message that Jesus' apostles confessed before Him near an empty tomb: "I know my Redeemer lives." It is not surprising that this reminder comes to me most often in the midst of a broken heart, shattered hopes, unseen tragedies, or a weakened spirit. But the last word is all we need to cling to. Through the good times and the bad, we can rest content knowing that we serve the very real, *living* God.

> *Therefore thus says the Lord God, See, I am laying in Zion a foundation stone, a tested stone, a precious cornerstone, a sure foundation: One who trusts will not panic.* —Isaiah 28:16

Zion was the hill on which King David built his palace; it later became a symbol of God's chosen people. When Christ came to establish the New Covenant, Zion became a symbol representing the firm foundation of God's Church and His heavenly city. Isaiah proclaims a promise of Christ as the only foundation of hope for escaping the wrath to come. This foundation was laid in Zion, in God's holy city: a stone, firm and able to support God's Church. It is a tried stone; a chosen stone approved of the Father and never failed any who made trial of it; a cornerstone, binding together the whole building and bearing the whole weight; precious in the sight of the Lord and of every believer; a sure foundation on which to build one's faith. The one who in any age or nation shall believe this testimony and rest all their hopes and their eternal soul on this foundation shall never be confounded. The right effect of faith in Christ is too quiet and calm the soul till events shall be timed by Him, who has all time in His own hands and power. Justification only comes through the righteousness of Christ; wisdom, strength, and holiness through the influences of the Holy Spirit; and happiness through the favor

41

of God. That protection in which one thought to shelter themselves will prove nothing more than a false hope when the day of judgment comes.

> *Therefore I have called her 'Rahab', who sits still.* —Isaiah 30:7

Rahab was often the name given to Egypt to describe a proud, arrogant, and selfish nation. "Oh, rebellious children," says the Lord, "who carry out a plan, but not mine; who make an alliance, but against my will, adding sin to sin" (Isaiah 30:1).

It was often the fault and folly of the Jews, that when troubled by their neighbors on one side, they sought assistance from others instead of looking up to God. This is what Isaiah is revealing to Israel: when we turn against each other, we commit one sin, and when we seek first for the refuge of others and not God's secure protection, we also commit sin, turning sin back-to-back, having no alliance but a sinful one. Our only hope -Isaiah reminds us- is to make the righteousness of God our refuge and seek for the sanctification of the Holy Spirit.

Humanity has always been prone to lean on its own understanding, but this will end in its shame and misery. As Isaiah warns, "Therefore the protection of Pharaoh shall become your shame; and the shelter in the shadow of Egypt your humiliation" (Isaiah 30:3). The riches so spent turned to a bad account. Men run into dangers of every kind when they forsake God to follow their carnal confidences. The Creator is the rock of the ages, the creator of a broken reed. We cannot expect too much from man or too little from God; our strength is in humble dependence upon God and His goodness, and quiet submission to His will. David reminds us of this quite clearly in the book of Psalms when he tells us "know that I am God!" (Psalm 46:10).

> *He will not always accuse, nor will he keep his anger forever. He does not deal with us according to our sins, nor repay us according to our iniquities. For as the heavens are high above the earth, so great is his steadfast love toward those who fear him; as far as the east is from the west, so far he removes our transgressions from us.*
> —Psalm 103:9-12

David reminds us what a great God we serve and how compassionate He is to His people. How weak and frail our body is and how sinful is our soul. God takes compassion on us; on those who fear His name. As a father has compassion on his child, so too does our heavenly Father look on us with kindly compassion and love, desiring to uplift the fallen and strengthen the weak. To this end, had God dealt with each of us according to our deeds and iniquities, we would have perished long ago; the deepest depth of Hell would be set aside for us. His anger against sin would grant to us the punishment we rightly deserve. Because God's grace and love are sufficient and everlasting to His people, the deeds of man are not held against him as a burden of sinfulness cast upon his shoulders. Our sinful acts and wicked ways deserve to be dealt with according to the measure of God's justice; our lot is set upon a far different measure of lovingkindness. Is this favor not undeserved? Our full praise and adoration shall be merited alone to the Lord, for He does not deal with us according to His justice but according to His love, mercy, and grace. "Bless the Lord, O my soul, and all that is within me, bless his holy name. Bless the Lord, O my soul, and do not forget all his benefits"— (Psalm 103:1-2)

> *Even though I walk through the darkest valley, I fear no evil; for you are with me; your rod and your staff— they comfort me.*
> —Psalm 23:4

The rod of God is the tool He uses to point out the lessons of life He wants us to learn: lessons of tribulation, sorrow, weeping, and so many more. But take heart, children of the living God! He sends many staffs that are strong and upright, staffs that we may surely lean upon. When I was in the hospital with severe brain cancer at the age of one, surely my parents and loved ones found this staff to lean upon: "For surely I know the plans I have for you, says the Lord, plans for your welfare and not for harm, to give you a future with hope" (Jeremiah 29:11).

For over a decade, I tried to fight traumatizing seizures, doubting they would ever come to an end. Time and time again I reminded myself of God's staff of encouragement: "In the world, you face persecution. But take courage; I have conquered the world!" (John 16:33). If God did not send His rod first, there would be no need for a staff to lean upon. It is *within* the lessons of life we learn from the Great Teacher, that He also equips us with His Word to lean upon during times of stumbling. Had God never let tribulations come to His children, we would never have come to appreciate the difficulties we face or understand His inner working of our soul. We would never hear His voice speaking to us in the quiet of our heart. God's desire for us to carry out His ministry and proclaim His majesty would not be fulfilled had it not been for the rod that points out the lessons of the Christian life. Our Father will never send us over the mountains without providing steady shoes to walk and His staff to lean upon.

And for this reason I suffer as I do. But I am not ashamed, for I know the one in whom I have put my trust, and I am sure that he is able to guard until that day what I have entrusted to him.
—1 Timothy 1:12

In the storms of life, we must put the ship (our soul) in one position and leave it there. We must secure our soul to the helm of God's faithfulness, His covenant promises, and His everlasting love through Christ. This Paul does; and as a result of setting his soul on the firm foundation in Christ, he was not ashamed to suffer for the Gospel truth. Two reasons he gives: he could suffer for the sake of Jesus because he knew Jesus, and Jesus' suffering gave Paul the power to "endure all things" (Philippians 4:13). Also, Paul was not ashamed to suffer because he trusted Christ, not his own efforts, to be the ultimate foundation. Let us secure our soul to this foundation in Christ, the only firm and sure foundation; then we too will not be reluctant to suffer for our Savior's sake and the Gospel truth.

A hero is not fed on sweets
Daily his own heart he eats
Chambers of the great are jails,
And headwinds right for royal sails.[3]

Cast your burden on the Lord, and he will sustain you; he will never permit the righteous to be moved. —Psalm 55:22

The burden of afflictions is very heavy, especially when combined with the temptations of Satan; there is also the burden of sin and corruption. The only relief under it is to look to Christ, who bore it (1 Peter 2:24). To "commit your way to the Lord" (Psalm 37:5) is to let Him do as seems good to Him and let us be satisfied. To cast our burden upon God is to rest upon His providence and promise; if we do so, He will carry us in the arms of His power and will strengthen our spirit by His Spirit, so that it shall sustain us through the trial. He will *never* suffer the righteous to be moved, to be so shaken by any troubles as to quit their duty to God or lose comfort in Him. He will not suffer them to be utterly cast down. He who bore the burden of our sorrows desires us to remember that He bears the burden of our cares that, as He knows what is best for us, He may provide it accordingly. Why do we not trust Christ to govern the world which He redeemed?

Consider the ravens: they neither sow nor reap, they have neither storehouse nor barn, and yet God feeds them. Of how much more value are you than the birds! And can any of you by worrying add a

---

[3] Emerson, Ralph Waldo. (n.d). *Streams in the Desert.*

44

single hour to your span of life? If then you are not able to do so small a thing as that, why do you worry about the rest? Consider the lilies, how they grow: they neither toil nor spin; yet I tell you, even Solomon in all his glory was not clothed like one of these. But if God so clothes the grass of the field, which is alive today and tomorrow is thrown into the oven, how much more will he clothe you—you of little faith! —Luke 12:24-28

There is scarcely any sin against which our Lord Jesus warns His disciples more than disquieting, distracting, and distrustful cares about the things of this life.

We must not value worldly possessions enough to worry about them. Fretting over such things will not bring them to us any quicker than if we were to leave such care in the hands of our Creator, which he implores us to do. Food, drink, clothing, and much more are mere provisions to the mortal body; we must value -above carnal desires- the eternal possessions of the soul. We must not set our mind on things that perish; such carnal desires satisfy for a day, but a nourished soul -clothed with the blood of Christ and fed with the blessings from Heaven- lives for eternity, knowing everlasting pleasure with God. Satisfying the soul in such a way, we are highly valued by our Maker; the very grasses of the field fall in awe, looking with wonder on the child of God.

The stone that the builders rejected has become the chief cornerstone. —Psalm 118:22

The building cannot stand without the cornerstone firmly set in its rightful place supporting the whole structure; just the same, the soul cannot stand without the cornerstone supporting the foundation against the spiritual storms of life. Christ is not just the rock, He is the cornerstone of our soul, holding it together so we may dwell safely forever in His love! Christ lays for us a firm foundation. Everything besides Christ is sand. Some build their hopes upon worldly prosperity, others upon an outward profession of religion, still others upon a worldly view of a successful vocation. Upon these they venture; but such foundations are all sand, too weak to bear such a fabric as our hopes of Heaven. There is a storm coming that will try every man's work. When God takes away the soul, where is the hope of the hypocrite? The house fell in the storm when the builder had most need of it and expected it would be a shelter to him. It fell when it was too late to build another. May the Lord make us wise builders for eternity, founding our house of hope and refuge solely in Him, then nothing shall separate us from the love of Christ Jesus.

Those who trust in the Lord are like Mount Zion, which cannot be moved, but abides forever. —Psalm 125:1

The image of eternal steadfastness: Mount Zion, eternal, neither bowing down nor moving to and fro. All those minds shall have truly stayed that are stayed on God. We shall be as Mount Zion: firm, a mountain supported by providence and divine promise. We cannot be removed from confidence in God; we abide forever in that grace which is the earnest of everlasting continuance in glory. Committing ourselves to God, we shall be safe from our enemies. God's covenant with His people cannot be broken, nor His care for us cease. Our troubles shall last no longer, yet our strength will bear us up under the troubles when they do come. Trusting God is a settling and establishing virtue. He who by His strength sets fast the mountains, by that same power stays the hearts of the ones that trust in Him. We too shall be as Mount Zion: firm, fixed, and stable.

Trust in the Lord with all you heart; and do not rely on your own insight. In all your ways acknowledge him, and he will make straight your paths. —Proverbs 3:5-6

When we lean on our own limited understanding and perceived wisdom, we will find a broken reed to lean upon, sure to fail; our attempts to lean on such a source are vain. It is sure that those who flourish lean only on the commandments, wisdom, and insight of the Lord. The one who looks not back but sees ahead will direct our paths to a sure and secure destination. We must trust our Maker that He will do what is best. In every situation -favorable or ill- we must acknowledge God with thankfulness. In all our ways that prove uncomfortable and that are hedged up with thorns, we must acknowledge Him with submission. Through all these times, surrendering reliance solely to God, acknowledging Him with all that happens in our life, it is promised that He will lead us on paths that are safe and good and happy, both for our lives and for His glory.

I can do all things through him who strengthens me.
—Philippians 4:13

Do not be misled to think of such statements as the means to get whatever you desire. Preceding this verse, Paul speaks of the very reason why he is able to do all things (vs. 12), and hereafter, why we are able to do all things. The apostle was often in bonds, imprisoned, and robbed of the mere necessities of life; but in all, he learned to bring his mind to his condition and make the best of it, not just leaning on God but learning to praise Him in every situation. Paul learned "to be content with whatever he had" (Philippians 4:11). Pride, unbelief, and vain hankering after something we do not have, and a fickle desire of present things make men discontented, even under favorable circumstances. Let us pray for patient submission and hope when we are abased, for humility and a heavenly mind when exalted. It is a special grace to have an equal temper of mind always. In a low state we cannot lose our comfort in God, nor distrust His providence, nor take any wrong course for our own supply, and in a prosperous condition, we cannot be proud or worldly.

Consider the work of God; who can make straight what he has made crooked? —Ecclesiastes 7:13

Often times God places us in deep difficulties and leads us into a corner from which there is no escape. We are often placed in situations where our judgments will not work. But God uses these circumstances of cloudiness to guide us to the other side. Our situation may seem filled with uncertainties, but it is just right; it is just where we need to be. The reason behind it will more than justify Him who brought us there and will be used as a platform for God to display His mighty power and grace. He will deliver us and imprint into our soul a lesson that we will not forget. We will be unable to thank God enough for what He has done.

And you shall tread down the wicked, for they will be ashes under the soles of your feet, on the day when I act, says the Lord of hosts. —Malachi 4:3

Malachi foreshadows the first and second comings of Christ: those who do wickedly, who do not fear God's anger, shall feel it. It is certainly to be applied to the Day of Judgment, when Christ shall be revealed in flaming fire to execute judgment on the proud and all that do wickedly. Christ is a rejoicing light to those who serve Him faithfully. Through Christ believers are justified and sanctified and so are brought to see the light. His influences render the sinner holy, joyful, and fruitful. The graces and comforts of the Holy Spirit are brought into the souls of men. Christ gave the Spirit to those who are His, to shine in their hearts and to be a comforter to them. That day, which to the wicked will burn as an oven, will to the righteous be bright as the morning. Another day is coming, far more dreadful to all that work wickedness than any which is gone before. How great then is the happiness of the believer, when he goes from the darkness and misery of this world to rejoice in the Lord forevermore!

Then he poured water into a basin and began to wash the disciples' feet and to wipe them with the towel that was tied around him. He came to Simon Peter, who said to him, 'Lord, are you going to wash

47

my feet?' Jesus answered, 'You do not know now what I am doing, but later you will understand.' —John 13:5-7

Christ washed His apostles' feet that He might signify to them the value of spiritual washing and the cleansing of the soul from the pollutions of sin. All those, and those alone, who are spiritually washed by Christ "in the blood of the Lamb" (Revelation 7:14) have a part with Christ. All whom Christ owns and saves, He justifies and sanctifies. The true believer is thus washed when he receives Christ for his salvation, and the same love which led Christ to wash the apostles' feet is still alive and active in us today through the power of the Holy Spirit.

There is a keynote that dwells much deeper than the physical act of Jesus washing the apostles' feet. When we think of the feet, a rather dirty thought comes to mind. Jesus thus symbolized the act of washing the apostle's feet as: by coming to Him, He may rid us of the dirty desires, thoughts, lusts, and emotions within us. Coming to Christ, He will wash us clean and set a new heart within us, one of purity in the Spirit, a heart of love, humility, and grace. The act of washing the apostles' feet symbolizes the deep desire Christ has to rid us of our old ways, washing us clean by the Holy Spirit.

Everyone then who hears these words of mine and acts on them will be like a wise man who built his house on rock. The rain fell, the floods came, and the winds blew and beat on that house, but it did not fall, because it had been founded on rock. —Matthew 7:24-25

Christ is not just the Rock; He is the Cornerstone of our soul, holding it together so we may dwell safely forever in His love! Christ lays for us a firm foundation. Everything besides Christ is sand. Some build their hopes on worldly prosperity, and others on an outward profession of religion. Upon these they venture; but such foundations are all sand, too weak to bear such a fabric as our hopes of Heaven. There is a storm coming that will try every person's work. When God takes away the soul, where is the hope of the hypocrite? The house fell in the storm when the builder had most need of it and expected it would be a shelter to him. It fell when it was too late to build another. May the Lord make us wise builders for eternity, founding our house of hope and refuge solely in Him, then nothing shall separate us from the love of Christ Jesus.

What then are we to say about these things? If God is for us, who is against us? —Romans 8:31

Paul speaks as one amazed and swallowed up in admiration, marveling at the height and depth and length and breadth of the love of Christ which surpasses knowledge. The only conclusion that Paul can make is to wonder in awe, asking and answering his own question that if God is for us, *none* can be against us. The more we know of other things, the less we wonder; but the further we are led into the Gospel mysteries, the more we are affected by them. This encourages our faith and hope. While God is for us, and we remain in His love, we may with a holy boldness defy all the powers of darkness.

> ***Therefore I am content with weakness, insults, hardships, persecutions, and calamities for the sake of Christ; for whenever I am weak, then I am strong.*** —2 Corinthians 12:10

When God does not take away our troubles and temptations but He gives grace enough for us to endure, we have no reason to complain. Grace signifies the goodwill of God toward us, and that is to enlighten and enliven us, sufficient to strengthen and comfort in all afflictions and distresses. His strength is made perfect in our weakness; His grace is manifested and magnified. When we are weak in ourselves, then we are strong in the grace of our Lord Jesus Christ. When we feel that we are weak in ourselves, we must go to Christ, receive strength from Him, and enjoy the supplies of divine strength and grace.

> ***The seventy returned with joy, saying, 'Lord, in your name even the demons submit to us!' He said to them, 'I watched Satan fall from heaven like a flash of lightning. See, I have given you authority to tread on snakes and scorpions, and over all the power of the enemy; and nothing will hurt you. Nevertheless, do not rejoice at this, that the spirits submit to you, but rejoice that your names are written in heaven.'*** —Luke 10:17-20

All our victories over Satan are obtained by power from Jesus Christ, and He must have all the praise. It was fit that particular notice should be taken of that hour of joy; in that hour in which Christ saw Satan fall and heard of the success of His ministers; in that hour He rejoiced. Another soul saved for Christ is another defeat over Satan; Christ watches him fall, and another name is written in the Lamb's Book of Life. Christ rejoices at the prospect of the salvation of many souls. Yet Christ has ever resisted the proud and given grace to the humble. Let us beware of spiritual pride, which has been the destruction of many. The more humble we become, the more we see how dependent we are on the teaching, help, and blessing of the Son of God; the more we shall know of both the Father and of the Son, the more blessed we shall be in seeing the glory and hearing the words of the divine Savior; and the more useful we shall be made in promoting His cause.

Chapter 7

God in Our Midst

But I see four men...and the fourth has the appearance of a god. —
Daniel 3:25

The comfort we find through Christ's truths teaches us freedom *in* affliction. The three men thrown into the fiery furnace had this comfort and peace, thus being able to withstand the furnace of affliction, not being hurt one bit by the flames. The fourth man, having "the appearance of a god," was the Lord, the Second Person of the Trinity, sent down to walk with the men in the furnace. While it is understood the Lord does not walk the Earth with us today, He has given to us the Holy Spirit to guide us, to walk with us in the flames and along the road of our life. By our afflictions, God's love and mercy comes to others. We become "more than conquerors" (Romans 8:37).

We serve as witnesses to God's unending gift of grace; in turn, the hearts of those still caught in the trap of sin are softened. God is able to work in their lives when their hearts are turned to the truth. It is not surprising that the king, astonished by what he had witnessed, made a decree that all worship only the one true God of Shadrach, Meshach, and Abednego (vs. 29). The shackles that bound Shadrach, Meshach, and Abednego also were removed in the furnace (vs. 27). These three men bound their hearts so firmly to God's truth of redemption that the shackles holding them bound were replaced with God's gifts of grace, mercy, and love. We too will come out of our blazing fires of trial and affliction, unshackled from our chains of doubt and despair, if only we bind our hearts tightly to God's promises of redemption and deliverance from the flames.

All this took place to fulfill what had been spoken by the Lord through the prophet: 'Look, the virgin shall conceive and bear a son, and they shall name him Emmanuel.' — Matthew 1:22-23

The prophecy is so solemn; the sign is so marked as given by God Himself (Isaiah 7:14). It must have raised high hopes for believers. And if the prospect of the coming of the divine Savior was a never-failing support to the hopes of ancient believers, what cause have we to be thankful that the Word was made flesh? For onto *us* the Messiah *was* born (Luke 2:11), and we cannot be destroyed while that blessing is in us. The strongest consolations in times of trouble are derived from Christ, our relation to Him, our interest in Him, and our expectations of and from Him. He would grow up like other children; but He would, unlike other children, uniformly refuse the evil and choose the good. And although His birth was by the power of the Holy Spirit, He would not feed on angel's food but drink the milk of sinners. This event marked the beginning of salvation for God's people; He no longer would call us His people, but by the blood of His own Son, God would call us His children.

I will be like the dew to Israel. —Hosea 14:5

Each morning I step outside, walking through green grass filled with dew. The dew is nature's provision to refresh the face of the earth. It comes in the evening, and without the dew, vegetation would die. Just as the earth is refreshed by natural dew, so are God's children refreshed with the spiritual dew of Heaven. Many times, in God's Word, the effect of dew is used as a symbol to explain the work of the Spirit in our life; as Titus states, the heavenly dew is our "renewal by the Holy Spirit" (Titus 3:5). The spiritual dew given to us from God is like heavenly manna that gives us the energy to carry out our work each day. By receiving this renewal from the Holy Spirit each day, we will be pulsated in the divine life of God. We must wait quietly before our Lord until we feel saturated with His presence, being refreshed and energized with the Holy Spirit; then we can move forward to accomplish our duties for Christ. If God refreshes His earth each morning, will He, in the same way, refresh the soul?

Your servant has killed both lions and bears. —1 Samuel 17:36

It should serve as great inspiration and strength remembering how David trusted God. Through David's faithfulness in God, he was able to defeat a lion, bear, and the mighty Goliath. When lions came to destroy his flocks, it served as a great opportunity for David to prove God's faithfulness: the promise to never let His children fall into the hands of the enemy. If he would have faltered or his faith would have swayed so much as an inch, David may have missed this great opportunity from God and never have become the great king of Israel. Naturally, we see a lion only as a source of alarm. Yet every temptation and difficulty in our life -if received correctly- is an opportunity from our Lord to show others how faithful He is.

When the "lions" in life come to us, may we see them as opportunities from God -no matter how fierce they may seem on the outside- and learn to see God's glory underneath the outer covering of these lions. When we look toward God, our eyes are opened to see His glory, even in temptations, trials, dangers, and misfortunes. Every promise of Scripture is a letter from God;

51

however, not every promise of God pertains to each of us. In the Old Testament, God spoke His promises mainly through the prophets and His messenger angels. In David's case, God had spoken to him through Nathan, thus making a promise with David. In the New Testament, every promise God makes to His children by the blood of Christ reveals His love for each of us who are called His own in Christ. In any set circumstance of life, we may read His Word, claiming a certain promise that He has declared to His children, all those who come to Him with a sincere heart, seeking to be one with Him in Christ. However, our petition for Him to keep a selected promise may not always be in line with His will for each of us; thus, we cannot take Him for a liar or deceiver. Since the beginning of the world, God has kept every promise He has made. We need simply to persist for some time in genuine prayer, taking God at His word, but waiting and watching for His promise to be carried out according to His will, not our own.

There is nothing more beautiful, strong, and safe than having such a mindset when it comes to waiting on God's promises. When we depend upon God's Word, He will never cheat us or break His word. As the apostle Peter tells us, the everlasting faithfulness of God makes His promises "precious and very great" (2 Peter 1:4). Four pillars hold the foundation to genuine prayer: the first two are justice and holiness which will never allow God to deceive us. The third is goodness which will never allow God to forget. The fourth pillar is God's truth which will never allow Him to change, thus having signed His signature at the end of every promise made in His Holy Word.

I have set my bow in the clouds, and it shall be a sign of the covenant between me and the earth. —Genesis 9:13

The thicker the cloud, the brighter the rainbow in the cloud; thus, as threatening afflictions abound, encouraging consolations much more abound. The rainbow is the reflection of the beams of the sun shining upon or through the drops of rain. All the glories of the seals of the covenant are derived from Christ, the Son of righteousness; and He will shed glory on the tears of his saints. A bow can speak terror if it is a weapon, but this has neither string nor arrow; and a bow alone will do little harm. It is a bow, but it is directed upward, not toward the earth; for the seals of the covenant were intended to comfort, not to terrify. As God looks upon the bow, He will remember the covenant; so, should we, that we may be mindful of the covenant with faith and thankfulness. Without revelation, this gracious assurance could not be known, and without faith, it can be of no use to us; thus, it is as to the still greater dangers to which all are exposed, and as to the new covenant with its blessings.

> *They looked toward the wilderness, and the glory of the Lord appeared in the cloud.* — Exodus 16:10

After the storm, we need to learn to look for the silver lining of the storm cloud. A discouraged soul is helpless—neither "able to stand against the wiles of the devil" (Ephesians 6:11) nor able to prevail in prayer for others who are in the storm. Many times, we focus on the darkness around us; we do not see the Lord's light beyond the storm, the silver lining in the clouds.

> *God is in the midst of the city; it shall not be moved; God will help it when the morning dawns.* —Psalm 46:5

David paints a beautiful picture for us exalting the ever-present God we trust and serve. That God may be in our midst always, our Father sent His Son and the Son sent us the Holy Spirit; so, God Himself -the Holy Godhead- may always be present in our lives. If the sun rises in the morning, God sets forth another day prepared for us to glorify Him. This includes every hardship, struggle, and temptation; but we know God is always present in our lives, guiding us down the path He's set for us, carrying us through the trying moments, "a very present help in trouble" (Psalm 46:1). So, let us be "like Mount Zion which cannot be moved, but abides *forever*" (Psalm 125:1), knowing that God Himself is with us always. This truth is stated and repeated in Psalm 46: "The Lord of hosts is with us; the God of Jacob is our refuge" (vs. 7 and 11). Oh, that may we rejoice in a God who chooses to dwell with us.

> *Am I a God nearby, says the Lord, and not a God far off? Who can hide in secret places so that I cannot see them? says the Lord. Do I not fill heaven and earth? says the Lord.* —Jeremiah 23:23-24

Jeremiah gives a warning against the false prophets of that day, as opposed to the true prophets of the Lord. Will they never see what judgments they prepare for themselves? Let them consider what a vast difference there is between these prophecies and those delivered by the true prophets of the Lord. Let them not call their foolish dreams divine oracles. Men cannot be hidden from God's all-seeing eyes. Sin cannot be hidden from the One that sees all. He is equally God, and He is equally near. "Where can I go from Your Spirit? Or where can I flee from your presence?" (Psalm 139:7) We need to remember that God is as near to us as we allow Him to be. When we come to Christ, we come near to the Father; and as our relationship and faith in Him grows, we draw ever nearer to Him. Is it not this closeness we want with our Lord? Even in the times of darkness, when the shadows of doubt seem to draw so close to us, God draws even closer. "Nevertheless, I am continually with you; You have taken hold of my right hand." (Psalm 73:23)

> **The Lord, your God, is in your midst, a warrior who gives victory; he will rejoice over you with gladness, he will renew you in his love; he will exult over you with loud singing.** —Zephaniah 3:17

Before the glorious times foretold (vs. 8-16), believers would be sorrowful and objects of reproach (vs. 1-7). But the Lord will save the weakest believer and cause true followers of Christ to be greatly honored where they had been treated with contempt. One act of mercy and grace shall serve both to gather Israel out of their dispersions and to lead them to their own land. Then will God's Israel be made a name and praise to eternity. These events alone can fully answer the language of this prophecy.

Many are the troubles of the righteous, but they may rejoice in God's love. Surely our heart should honor the Lord and rejoice in Him when we hear such words of judgment and grace. If now kept from His ordinances, it is our trial and grief; but in due time we shall be gathered into His temple above. The glory and happiness of the believer will be perfect, unchangeable, and eternal when he is freed from earthly sorrows and brought to heavenly bliss. "Take heart, it is I; do not be afraid" (Matthew 14:27). He that comes to save is Jesus the Christ. Let us rejoice.

> **For God has done what the law, weakened by the flesh, could not do: by sending his own Son in the likeness of sinful flesh, and to deal with sin, he condemned sin in the flesh, so that the just requirement of the law might be fulfilled in us, who walk not according to the flesh but according to the Spirit.** —Romans 8:3-4

We cannot save ourselves. "Those who are in the flesh cannot please God" (vs. 8), Because the flesh has been weakened by the curse of sin, we cannot keep with the Mosaic Law. By His grace, God chose to save humanity, desiring not only that His created people would live in freedom from the damnation of a law that could not be kept, but also to prove His sovereignty and power over Satan and the grave. Jesus the Christ came in the likeness of a mortal, fleshly body, yet one without sin (Hebrews 4:15), that by His sacrifice we would not be damned to keep the law in the flesh. God did this because it was necessary to fulfill the law's requirement of death for sin and life for righteousness. Paul reminds us in Romans 8 that coming to Christ, one is baptized by His Spirit. Being baptized into the Spirit, one lives for the future good of God's perfect will (Romans 8:5). "But if Christ is in you, though the body is dead because of sin, the Spirit is life because of righteousness" (Romans 8:10). May we come to Christ, being baptized by His Spirit, not only being freed from the damnation of the law but living out a life for God's perfect and sinless will. Besides Him, there is *no one* able to save (Isaiah 43:11).

Now may the Lord of peace himself give you peace at all times and in all ways. The Lord be with all of you. —2 Thessalonians 3:16

-And-

Come to me, all you that are weary and are carrying heavy burdens, and I will give you rest. —Matthew 11:28

Peace is found in the presence of the Lord. We will never truly obtain peace if we continue to look to what pleases the flesh (Romans 8:6). We need nothing more than the presence of the Lord; this is all in all what makes us happy; in every situation, in each circumstance, no matter who is absent, if God is present, we will find and know peace with Him through Christ. We are each called to the same eternal happiness: "peace with God through our Lord Jesus Christ" (Romans 5:1). Although this eternal peace is our end prize, the way to obtain it in this life is through faith and trust in the One who gives us the opportunity to grasp that peace. Those whose mind stays focused on Him will forever remain in perfect peace (Isaiah 26:3). Let the peace of God rule in your soul; it is His working in all who are His. "*He offers us peace in the face of uncertainty, hope in exchange for heaviness.*"[4] *Max Lucado* encourages us to "reach out and grasp this peace and hold it close to our hearts."

Though I have afflicted you, I will afflict you no more. —Nahum 1:12

There is a limit to God's afflictions; He gives them and in time takes them away. We needn't complain, wondering when the afflictions and hardships will end. We must quietly wait, patiently enduring the will of our Lord until He returns. "For he does not willingly afflict or grieve anyone" (Lamentations 3:33). God removes His rod when His purpose in using it has been accomplished. If our afflictions are sent only to test us so that we may yield glory to Him, they will end only when we testify to Him all the glory and honor. The point at which we reflect Christ's image is the point at which the storms of tribulation cease.

Trials serve to purify and refine our faith within. Troubles are necessary for all the saints of God. Many times, God lets us come to the precipice of our trouble so that we may learn the calm of God's promise to never leave or forsake us (Hebrews 13:5); He will never let His beloved fall. He lets us come to the cliff, only to offer His grace and peace of knowing that if we trust faithfully in Him, He will pull us back from the edge. God sends His

---

[4] Lucado, Max. (1984, rev 2012). *In the Eye of the Storm.* Thomas Nelson publisher.

clouds; He can just as easily send the stars. Just as He has set the rough waves upon the great waters, He will surely open a sea of glass.

> *I will make them and the region around my hill a blessing; and I will send down the showers in their season; they shall be showers of blessing. The trees of the field shall yield their fruit, and the earth shall yield its increase. They shall be secure on their soil; and they shall know that I am the Lord, when I break the bars of their yoke, and save them from the hands of those who enslaved them.*
> — Ezekiel 34:26-27

The prophet speaks of Christ and of the most glorious times of His Church on earth. Under Him as the Good Shepherd, the Church will be a blessing to all around. Christ is as a tender plant out of dry ground, strongly resembling the Tree of Life, bearing all the fruits of salvation. He yields spiritual food to the souls of His people. Our constant desire and prayer should be that there may be showers of blessings in every place where the truth of Christ is preached and that all who profess the Gospel may be filled with fruits of righteousness.

> *See, I am sending my messenger ahead of you, who will prepare your way; the voice of one crying out in the wilderness: 'Prepare the way of the Lord, make his paths straight.'* —Mark 1:2-3

Who was this voice? This was the voice of John the Baptist, referencing the prophet Isaiah, speaking of Jesus Christ who was to come after him, one much greater and majestic: one to whom "I am not worthy to stoop down and untie the thong of his sandals" (Mark 1:7). Isaiah and Malachi each spoke concerning the beginning of the Gospel of Jesus Christ (Isaiah 40:3, Malachi 3:1). From these prophets we may observe that Christ comes among us, bringing with Him a treasure of grace and a scepter of government.

John prepared a way for Christ to come into the world by preaching repentance, thus Christ would have a way to come into the heart. John administered the ordinance of baptism, that believers would be baptized by the Holy Spirit when Christ came. We must prepare a way for Christ, repenting of our sins, ridding ourselves of our old ways and laying aside any sentiments contrary to Him. Christ's Kingdom on earth must be set forth by the teaching of His Word and the convictions of the Spirit, that high and proud thoughts may be brought down and good desires planted in their place. Hard hearts may be humbled and all hindrances removed. The ministry of John has been used as an instrument to proclaim Christ's coming, that we may be ready for His Kingdom and will on earth, as it is in Heaven.

Why do you look for the living among the dead? —Luke 24:5

The resurrection is a joy to all Christ's faithful followers, but a terrifying fear to His enemies and those who oppose the truth of the empty tomb. Christ's children know and serve a living Savior. By the truth of the empty tomb, we have a taste of God's divine nature. He was always alive as God, but now He is alive as man also. The flesh tastes not the death He once died for us so that through His resurrection, we will not know the death that once waited at the door. To the benefit and advantage of His redeemed ones -the ones that hold the faith that He was truly God- we can and will proclaim that He *is* truly the Son of God, to make intercession for His beloved and give them means of justification. We are partakers in an endless life with our Savior. We too will see the light through a darkened grave if we but remember and accept the promise God left us: that "I conquered death!" We will no longer search for the dead amongst the living; we seek the One that lives forevermore! He is not the great "I was" but the great "*I Am.*" Only because He lives, we live! "I was dead, and see, I am alive forever and ever" (Revelation 1:18).

But our citizenship is in heaven, and it is from there that we are expecting a Savior, the Lord Jesus Christ. —Philippians 3:20

It was from this heavenly place alone that the Savior would come; for one that could not sin was He alone who has the power to destroy the damnation of sin set upon the flesh of fallen humanity. The place we truly belong is with our Maker in a heavenly place; earth is set to be that heavenly realm, for it is where God dwells that is the heavenly home. By the downfall of the curse and the scar of sin left upon the world, we are set here that by God's grace, He may teach us a brighter road to follow, thus coming closer to Him by nothing but the sacrifice of His Son, that His family may grow here, that we all may abide in our spiritual home with the Lord forever, the place in which we were made to stay. Pick up your permanent residence and make it be in Heaven. Wherever you live in this life should remain of small interest to your heart, knowing that the end prize is to be with God forever where He dwells. All who have given their life to Christ are destined to be with Him forevermore in the Heavenly realm; that is to be the believer's true resting place. Our residency is to be with God where He is, and wherever He is, that is the heavenly place.

Then he said to Thomas, 'Put your finger here and see my hands. Reach out your hand and put it in my side. Do not doubt but believe.' Thomas answered him, 'My Lord and my God!' Jesus said to

him, 'Have you believed because you have seen me? Blessed are those who have not seen and yet have come to believe.'
—John 20:27-29

Although the phrase "doubting Thomas" is known and used by many, Thomas himself cannot be singled out as a sceptic. John includes this story in his Gospel as a means to teach his readers a lesson taught by Christ Himself: "blessed are those who do not see and yet believe" (vs. 29). The evangelist includes the story of Thomas in order to encourage all those people of the present and future ages who come to believe in the Lord without seeing Him. The people of this category are called blessed because they have reached an enhanced spiritual level, being led by the Holy Spirit. Eventually, this faith becomes trust, which is "reckoned to him as righteousness" (Romans 4:22). The Holy Spirit was poured out by Christ on His Church, endowing her and the believers with extraordinary gifts and amazing experiences. This same Spirit gives us the proofs that we long for; the proofs written in His Holy Word and lived by Christ Himself. To look for further signs and evidence would be wrong, yet some are demanding miracles, faith-healings, visions, voices, impressions, transports, depressions, or the like; such demands are dishonoring to the Lord. God keeps the physical evidence away from us until we learn to trust Him without it, i.e., coming to the point of trusting in the grace of the Holy Spirit. True faith focuses on the unseen; it brings us to the end of our own strength and teaches us that we must rely solely on God.

To one who has faith, no explanation is necessary. To one without faith, no explanation is possible. —Thomas Aquinas.

We honor God when we walk by faith. In the church today there are many doubting souls, slow to believe, suspicious, critical, and doubting God's Holy Word and His promises made therein; yet we must take heart. The faithful are to uplift and support the weak, helping them come to a full understanding of Christ.

Chapter 8

Union with the Divine

He will be called Son of God. **— Luke 1:35**

Being sinners in the presence of the sinless Lord, far as the curse of that burden weighs on humanity, we could not be saved by human flesh alone but by God Himself through the divine act of grace. This child must be born miraculously: born of the flesh, yet keeping the union with the Most High, in the presence of the Holy Spirit, thus the holy God-head becoming one with humanity, yet keeping the divine nature of one free from sin: being the Son of God and the Son of man. The name given to him, Emmanuel (God with us), would forever hold the truth of the extraordinary act of God becoming one with His people.

> *I have said this to you, so that in me you may have peace. In the world you face persecution. But take courage; I have conquered the world!* —John 16:33

The whole purpose of Christ's coming was not simply to make amends for our sinfulness, but to turn humanity toward the Father, to lead us away from deceit and lust to peace and communion with Him. While being born anew in Christ, our old self is done away with, and we are led by the grace of the Father and Christ's Holy Spirit to also trample Satan's temptations as our Lord did. Trials still alarm us, temptations still await us, and Satan still waits at the door for us to answer; but with Christ, we too overcome the world and become "more than conquerors" (Romans 8:37). Instead of trials, setbacks, and persecutions, we learn to see our Lord through it all, and we too overcome the world with Christ. "For whatever is born of God conquers the world. And this is the victory that conquers the world, our faith" (1 John 5:4).

> *Let him kiss me with the kisses of his mouth! For your love is better than wine, your anointing oils are fragrant, your name is perfume poured out; therefore, the maidens love you.* —Song of Solomon 1:2-3

Solomon's song resembles the relationship between God and Israel, and hereafter, the relationship between Christ and His children. The believer speaks in the character of the spouse of the King (the Messiah). The assurances of pardon with which believers are favored fill them with peace and joy in believing, causing them to abound in hope by the power of the Holy Spirit come upon them from God as the very kisses from Him to His child. Gracious souls take great pleasure in loving Christ and being loved by Him. Christ's love is more valuable and desirable than the best this world can give. The name of Christ is not like ointment sealed up but like ointment poured forth, which denotes the freeness and fullness of the setting forth of His grace by the Gospel. Those who He has redeemed and sanctified are like virgins that love Jesus Christ and "follow the Lamb wherever he goes" (Revelation 14:4).

> *What I say to you in the dark, tell in the light; and what you hear whispered, proclaim from the housetops. Do not fear those who kill the body but cannot kill the soul; rather fear him who can destroy both soul and body in hell.* —Matthew 10:27-28

The mystery of God's divine plan (long-held secret) was then to be published, to be made known to all people. In the same way, Jesus commissioned His apostles, so too He commissions us to make known the mysteries God reveals to us in the quiet of our heart, and proclaim from the highest heights the soft whispers of the Spirit spoken in our ears.

God desires not that His Word be held back from the hearts of men; He asks that we proclaim His truths of love and grace to all generations, sowing the seed of peace in each heart. The early followers of Christ suffered much to proclaim these truths. Many of them gave their very lives in ransom to proclaim Christ's kingdom. These early evangelists did not fear the death of the body; they confirmed to continue to preach the truth that seeds be sown and souls be saved. We must confirm to proclaim the truths of God's love, being "doers of the word, and not merely hearers who deceive themselves" (James 1:22). May we not deceive ourselves or those around us, but proclaim the good news of God's grace.

> *Who is that coming up from the wilderness, leaning upon her beloved? Under the apple tree I awakened you. There your mother was in labor with you; there she who bore you was in labor. Set me as a seal upon your heart, as a seal upon your arm; for love is strong as death, passion fierce as the grave. Its flashes are flashes of fire, a raging flame.* —Song of Solomon 8:5-6

The Jewish Church came up from the wilderness, supported by divine power and favor. The Christian Church was raised from a low, desolate condition by the grace of Christ relied upon. Believers, by the power of grace, are brought up from the wilderness. A wilderness state is a sinful state in which there is no true comfort; it is a wandering, wanting state. There is no coming out of this wilderness but by leaning on Christ as our Beloved, by faith; not leaning to our own understanding, nor trusting in any righteousness of our own, but in the strength of Him *who is our righteousness*. The words of the Church to Christ that follow entreat an abiding place in His love and protection by His power: ***Set me as a seal upon your heart; let me always have a place in your heart; let me have an impression of love upon your heart***. Of this the soul would be assured; and without such knowledge, no rest is to be found. Those who truly love Christ are jealous of everything that would draw them from Him. If we love Christ, the fear of coming short of His love or the temptations to forsake Him will be most painful to us. No waters can quench Christ's love for us, nor will any floods drown it. May our love for Christ be as His love is to us: a flame of fire that cannot be quelled.

> ***People were bringing even infants to him that he might touch them; and when the disciples saw it, they sternly ordered them not to do it. But Jesus called for them and said, 'Let the little children come to me, and do not stop them; for it is to such as these that the kingdom of God belongs. Truly I tell you, whoever does not receive the kingdom of God as a little child will never enter it.'*** —Luke 18:15-17

A child has a stilled and quiet soul, unable to grasp pride, anger, or deceit. A child has clinging trust; one can hope no more than to be safe in his mother's arms. This type of trust is what we are to bring before our Lord; to know no other than to live a life of trust in Him. It is with such attitude and gentility of heart that we are to enter the kingdom. The gate to Heaven is low; those who hold their head high, relying on and trusting in themselves, will never enter through this gate. A child's clinging trust becomes a man's valued virtue: the character we must have to enter through the gate of Heaven.

> ***For those whom he foreknew he also predestined to be conformed to the image of his Son.*** —Romans 8:29

We are to be conformed to the image of Christ; this is the Father's ultimate purpose for all of His children. Think on this after looking back at Paul's statement in verse 28. From the beginning, God desired that He would have a heavenly kingdom on earth, with His children bearing the perfect resemblance of His own Son: children who imitate the faith and obedience which Christ showed while He lived on earth. Christ came not only to offer us redemption from sin and communion with the Father but also, He came as the perfect image of the Father, that by reflecting Christ, the Father may also be seen in His children. God means to break us off from sin, bringing us nearer to Himself, weaning us from the world and fitting us for Heaven. It is a call from self and earth to the Father and Jesus Christ, and Heaven as our eternal end, from sin and vanity to grace and holiness as our way. This is the Gospel call. The love of God ruling in the hearts of those who were once enemies to Him proves that they have been called according to His purpose: to be His own. None are justified but those who accept the call of Christ to come near; those who stand out against the Gospel call abide only under the guilt of God's wrath. The power of corruption is broken through Christ, and the guilt of sin removed in justification. Nothing can come between the soul of one saved and eternal glory. This encourages our faith and hope. From this point forward, our heavenly Father is working in our heart, purifying our soul, and strengthening our faith so that we too may bear the resemblance of the Son.

All that God designed for glory and happiness as the end, He decreed that grace and holiness be the way. What better way to help guide us toward grace and holiness than by the guidance of Christ's Holy Spirit?

I therefore, the prisoner in the Lord, beg you to lead a life worthy of the calling to which you have been called, with all humility and gentleness, with patience, bearing with one another in love, making every effort to maintain the unity of the Spirit in the bond of peace. There is one body and one Spirit, just as you were called to the one hope of your calling, one Lord, one faith, one baptism, one God and Father of all, who is above all and through all and in all. — Ephesians 4:1-6

While many in today's world are engaged in celebrating diversity, the Bible places an extraordinary emphasis on the value of unity. The Persons of the Godhead are a grand tri-unity of absolute perfection. Paul stresses the word "one" and uses it to describe the unity we are to have with our brothers and sisters, just as the Godhead is united as one; being many, yet God unites Himself as one and all, Lord over all. In this same way, we are many children but all part of the same family; that is why Paul urges us to keep the unity of the Spirit alive. Reading these verses, one phrase comes to mind: "United we stand; divided we fall!" We can either live as one family in Christ or strive for diversity and fall to Satan, hindering God's work in our life and further drawing others away from Christ. The bond of peace in Christ unites us as one; the peace He freely offers. Brothers and sisters, as one Church we are bound in unity as one body in Christ, thus having one calling, to be sanctified as one in the Spirit. Although Paul only mentions four fruits of the Spirit (vs. 2), we are to live out each fruit of the Spirit, showing our tolerance and love for each member of Christ's Church; and thereafter being as one body in Christ -love all of God's people-. Our Savior sums it up nicely when he reminds us: "You shall love the Lord your God with all your heart" and, "You shall love your neighbor as yourself" (Matthew 22:37&39). We are to walk in unity with other Christians, binding our differences together as one, working for the good of Christ's Church.

> *The Lord was very angry with your ancestors. Therefore, say to them, thus says the Lord of hosts: Return to me, says the Lord of hosts, and I will return to you, says the Lord of hosts.*
> — Zechariah 1:2-3

Of the hosts above and below, of angels and of men, of Heaven and earth and all that is therein, God's almighty power and sovereign dominion should engage and encourage sinners to repent and turn to Him. It is very desirable to have the Lord of hosts for our friend and very dreadful to have Him for our enemy. Observe the message God sent by His servants the prophets to our fathers: turn now from your evil ways and from your evil doings. Be persuaded to leave your sins as the only way to prevent eternal ruin. To leave sin behind and follow God: this was the way He asks the Israelites to follow, and He asks us also to follow the only way that leads to Him.

> *At three o'clock Jesus cried out with a loud voice, 'Eloi, Eloi, lema sabachthani?' which means, 'My God, my God, why have you for-saken me?'*—Mark 15:34

This was not a simple cry of lamentation or pouring out of pity when being left alone to die on the cross; this was abandonment from the Father. The divine love between Father and Son was broken at Cavalry's cross, as Christ Jesus was sacrificed for the penalty of sinners. The floodgates of the Father's wrath were poured out in fullness upon His Son. He turned His face from sin; the wrath thrust upon the shoulders of His sinless Son. Yet the One who looks on sin with scornful wrath looks on us with love and grace, as the price for sin was paid in full. The Father chose to abandon His Son so that through Christ, He will never abandon us. Instead of our sin, God sees His Son.

> *When Jesus had received the wine, he said, 'It is finished.' Then he bowed his head and gave up his spirit.* —John 19:30

It is finished! The fate of this fallen world and the corruption of a sinful people were washed away in the blood of Christ. The Old Testament proph-ecies concerning the long-awaited Messiah -come to save not only the Jews but all people- were fulfilled. The law was broken and restored with an ever-lasting law of redemption from sin. Death was done away with. Paths of darkness were abandoned, and light shown through the clouds of a darkened world. The counsels concerning the suffering of a sinful people were now laid down forever upon the cross, taken for us by Christ. The fear of death was conquered through an empty tomb; and life's uncertainties were renewed by God's grace, mercy, and peace. Shadows were done away, and an end was made of all transgressions. The work of our redemption and salvation was now completed. Christ's life was freely given up to make amends for the sins of humanity. The wages of sin was no longer death but communion with the Father. Life and death were conquered, both for this world and the next.

And now faith, hope, and love abide, these three; and the greatest of these is love. —1 Corinthians 13:13

-And-

Beloved, let us love one another, because love is from God; everyone who loves is born of God and knows God. Whoever does not love does not know God, for God is love. —1 John 4:7-8

Faith fixes on the divine revelation and assents thereto, relying on the divine Redeemer. Hope fastens on future happiness and waits for that, but in Heaven faith will be swallowed up in actual sight and enjoyment. There is no room to believe and hope when we can see and enjoy. But there, love will be made perfect; there we shall perfectly love God, and there we shall perfectly love one another. "So, we have known and believe the love that God has for us. God is love, and those who abide in love abide in God, and God abides in them" (1 John 4:16).

O Lord, who may abide in your tent? Who may dwell on your holy hill? —Psalm 15:1-5

Those who walk blamelessly, and do what is right, and speak the truth from their heart; who do not slander with their tongue, and do no evil to their friends, nor take up a reproach against their neighbors; in whose eyes the wicked are despised, but who honor those who fear the Lord; who stand by their oath even to their hurt; who do not lend money at interest, and do not take a bribe against the innocent. Those who do these things shall never be moved." The way to Heaven, if we would be happy, we must be holy; we are encouraged to walk in that way. It is the happiness of glorified saints that they dwell on the holy hill; they are at home there; they shall be forever there. These characteristics of the holy seem impossible to the human heart; for we yet live in a world cast down and darkened by the curse of sin. To be purified and holy, to dwell on God's holy hill, seems but a dream of the downfallen, a song sung by sinners. How to accomplish this task, how to walk blamelessly before the Lord, and purify our heart with the sinless actions hereby mentioned, David proceeds to answer, that the Lord alone is our refuge; apart from Him there is no good (Psalm 16:1-2). Those alone who take refuge

64

solely in the character, love, mercy and grace of the Lord will find a secure refuge to plant their soul. In God alone, one will taste the sweetness of living a holy and blameless life. Every true living member of the Church -like the Church itself- is built upon a rock. The one that achieves these characteristics of holiness shall not be moved forever; the grace of God shall always be sufficient for them.

Now, however, that you have come to know God, or rather to be known by God, how can you turn back again to the weak and beggarly elemental spirits? How can you want to be enslaved to them again? —Galatians 4:9

We know God only because He first knew us. We come to God because He first longed to take us in as His sons and daughters. Before Christ knew us, we worshipped idols and craved sin and were subject to God's wrath. But He calls us home, and to go home to Him is to go home to the salvation of our soul. But nothing is more grievous to God than a faithful heart that has gone cold. Do we labor in vain, only to plant seeds in cold hearts? Do we turn aside from this race to be enslaved by the lusts of this world? "What has become of the goodwill you felt?" (Galatians 4:15). Have you forgotten all of the blessings our Father pours out from Heaven? We have only to set our eyes to focus on Christ, our heart to know none other than the love of Christ, and our soul to be enslaved with Christ. Thus, we will be children of God, "and if children, then heirs, heirs of God and joint heirs with Christ -if, in fact, we suffer with him so that we may also be glorified with him" (Romans 8:17). Let us not turn aside from what we have come to know, nor grow weary of the faith that has been planted in our soul. "For we will reap at harvest time, if we do not give up" (Galatians 6:9).

At that moment the curtain of the temple was torn in two, from top to bottom. The earth shook, and the rocks were split. The tombs also were opened, and many bodies of the saints who had fallen asleep were raised. After his resurrection they came out of the tombs and entered the holy city and appeared to many. Now when the centurion and those with him, who were keeping watch over Jesus, saw the earthquake and what took place, they were terrified and said, 'Truly this man was God's Son!' —Matthew 27:51-54

A curtain serves as a cover. Until the time of Christ's death, the way to the Father was covered by the sin of humanity. By His death, Christ opened the way to the Father. We have an open way through Christ to the throne of grace now and to the throne of glory hereafter. The graves of many saints who slept in Christ were opened; following Christ's resurrection, they too were raised to life again. This was a proof of Christ's power over death and the grave. By dying, He through death destroyed him that had the power over it and abolished death itself, becoming the plague of death and the destruction of the grave, taking into His hands the keys of death and Hades. We too may find comfort in this: that we who are saints with Christ will conquer the grave, rising to a new life in Him.

The dreadful appearances of God in His providence sometimes work strangely for the conviction and awakening of sinners. This was expressed in the terror that fell upon the centurion and the Roman soldiers. Never were the horrid nature and effects of sin so tremendously displayed as on that day when the beloved Son of the Father died upon the cross, suffering for sin, the just for the unjust, that He might bring us to God our Father. When we see Him who was crucified, our stubborn and hard hearts will split, as the very rocks of the earth; then we too like the Roman guards will proclaim "surely this man *is* the Son of God!" Let us, with an eye of faith, behold Christ and Him crucified, and be affected with that great love by which He loves us.

> *And they clothed him in a purple cloak; and after twisting some thorns into a crown, they put it on him. And they began saluting him, 'Hail, King of the Jews!' They struck his head with a reed, spat upon him, and knelt down in homage to him.* — Mark 15:17-19

The cross and shame are put together. God having been dishonored by the sin of humanity; Christ made satisfaction by submitting to the greatest disgrace of human nature. It was a cursed death. The Roman soldiers mocked our Lord Jesus Christ as a King in the same way the high priests had mocked Him as a prophet and savior. Purple or scarlet -the color of pride, majesty, and honor- worn by kings, was made into a robe of shame to Christ. He wore the crown of thorns which we deserved, that we might wear the crown of glory which He merited. We were by sin liable to all shame and contempt; but to deliver us, the Lord Jesus submitted to that very shame and contempt. The sufferings of the meek and holy Redeemer are ever a source of instruction to the believer. Jesus thus suffered; and shall I, a vile sinner, fret or complain? Shall I indulge anger, or utter reproaches and threats because of troubles and injuries? The shame, hurt, and injustices we endure -if endured in the right way, through Christ- will become for us songs of praise.

> *See, I have inscribed you on the palms of my hands; your walls are continually before me.* —Isaiah 49:16

Be assured that God has tender affection for His church and people; He would not have them to be discouraged. God's compassions to His people infinitely exceed those of the most tender of parents toward their children. His setting them as a mark on His hand or a seal upon His arm denotes His being ever mindful of them. As far as we have scriptural evidence -and the baptism of the Spirit- that we belong to His ransomed flock, we may be sure that He will never forsake us. Let us then give due diligence to make our calling and election sure and rejoice in the hope and glory of God.

> *For through the law I died to the law, so that I might live to God. I have been crucified with Christ; and it is no longer I who live, but it is Christ who lives in me. And the life I now live in the flesh I live by faith in the Son of God, who loved me and gave himself for me. I do not nullify the grace of God; for if justification comes through the law, then Christ died for nothing.* —Galatians 2:19-21

The point that Paul is trying to get across to his readers is the sharp contrast between the Law of Moses and the faith in Jesus Christ. He draws this conclusion from the truth he declares in Romans 6:6, "We know that our old self was crucified with him." For us, then, being crucified with Christ, we die to sin but are alive in the Lord. The old person is done away, replaced by the person in the flesh who lives by faith in Christ, only to have Him reflected in his life. Believers find themselves living a life dependent on Christ. We are no longer slaves to sin but rather slaves to Christ, to live only to bring the Father glory. Yet slaves, we are free, free from the authority of the law, free from the damnation of sin, and free from the wrath of God. Our life becomes subject to God's good pleasure. The new body we live in is that of our Savior reflected in us, and our soul finds the satisfaction and bliss of the grace of God.

> *Your mother and your brothers are standing outside, wanting to see you." But he said to them, 'My mother and my brothers are those who hear the word of God and do it.'* —Luke 8:20-21

The true kindreds of Christ are the ones that take to heart the true meaning of the Christmas story and desire to share its mysteries and truths with others. Jesus is pointing to the completion of His Family by the devotion of unison. He lives in unison with the Divine; He desires that we too may live in unison with Him, thus living in unison with our fellow followers of Christ. Becoming one with Christ, we thus become one with the Divine, hereafter becoming one with our brothers and sisters in Christ. Devotion to God creates an incomparable bond that exceeds family and friends! The closer we draw to Christ, the closer we draw to each other! As we use our gifts for the glory of God and the benefit of our brethren, further will they be provided to us, thus being further profitable for the glory of God. Great encouragement is given to those who prove themselves faithful hearers of the Word, by being doers of the work; Christ owns them as His relations. Let us cease from men and cleave to Christ; let us look upon each of Christ's children -in whatever condition of life- as the brother or sister of the Lord.

I do not call you servants any longer, because the servant does not know what the master is doing; but I have called you friends, because I have made known to you everything that I have heard from my Father. —John 15:15

Once we were slaves to our sin and set apart from the Divine. Jesus gives us a chance for an intimate friendship with Him; "You did not choose me but I chose you" (John 15:16). To become the sin of sinners, He now calls us His friends: no longer slaves to sin or servants of Satan. May we desire such a friendship, coming to Christ with open heart, as His arms remain always open wide to receive us. Being children of the Father, we are thus friends of Jesus the Christ; and through His Holy Spirit, He has made known to us the hidden mysteries of the Father.

May I never boast of anything except the cross of our Lord Jesus Christ, by which the world has been crucified with me, and I to the world. —Galatians 6:14

Being one with Christ, we are prisoners with Him, thus crucified with Christ. We must let go of the love we greedily hold for the world. Proud, hard, and sinful hearts will be content to put on a good act of belief to bring praise and glory to themselves. Hardened hearts become deceived by the lust and greed to boast of such things of this world as a good reputation, or being known as religious. Such carnal desires and lusts weigh on and pull at the heart, dragging it further to Sheol. These things of the world eventually come to an end; they are only temporal. Outward professions and carnal desires will never stand the test. The heart converted by Christ allows us to yearn for our Maker. We are less likely to love this world when we have considered the crucified Redeemer. Let us remain crucified to this world and boast of the holy death, resurrection, and life of our Lord Jesus Christ, through whom we receive life eternal.

Jesus, full of the Holy Spirit, returned from the Jordan and was led by the Spirit in the wilderness, where for forty days he was tempted by the devil. —Luke 4:1-2

The strongest forces of temptation often come upon us when we are closest to God. When our faith shakes the very forces of hell, Satan aims high to stop us. When we have the fullness of God's Spirit, we will always experience great conflicts with temptation. God allows temptation because it does for our faith what a storm does for an oak tree: rooting it deeper into firm ground. There is a tremendous strength for us when we are gripped tightly to Christ and Him to us. It is during the times of temptation -when Satan uses all his forces to pull us away- that we feel Christ's tug to hold us back. It is in the complete darkness of temptation and sin that we see Christ's light shining the brightest!

> *Child, remember that during your lifetime you received your good things, and Lazarus in like manner evil things; but now he is comforted here, and you are in agony.* —Luke 16:25

Those who abide not in Christ, though they may flourish for a while in outward profession, yet come to nothing. It is no use living in splendor in this life when one's soul is far from God; there will be no splendor in the life to come. "You are those who justify yourselves in the sight of others; but God knows your hearts; for what is prized by human beings is an abomination in the sight of God" (Luke 16:15). The love for such earthly things such as wealth will only separate a heart further from God. Jesus warns us: "No slave can serve two masters; for a slave will either hate the one and love the other, or be devoted to the one and despise the other. You cannot serve God and wealth" (Luke 16:13). We will either become slaves to our sin, seeking after such carnal desires as the world can offer, or prisoners with Christ to serve God alone. It is most profitable to be rich in spiritual blessings God offers through His endless grace.

> *Jesus answered them, 'Destroy this temple, and in three days I will raise it up.'* —John 2:19

-And-

> *Don't you know that you yourselves are God's temple and that God's Spirit dwells in your midst?* —1 Corinthians 3:16

The Temple was the very place where God was worshiped. As a symbolic metaphor of His resurrection, Jesus spoke of the Temple of His body, as He gave Himself up for us, degrading Himself to great humiliation, being brought so low as to be marked along with the transgressors (Isaiah 53:12) and sinners on our behalf, that by His blood shed we may be marked amongst the holy. Calling that place His Father's house (vs. 16), the Jews sought a sign of Jesus that He may have such authority to clear the Temple. The night of His crucifixion, they not only mock Him, but also would not believe until He came down from the cross (Mark 15:32), knowing that if Jesus' claim were true, only He would have such power to come down. This was not His sign to give. He gave a much more convincing sign three days later when He conquered the grave, not only fulfilling their wish for a sign but proving that He *is* the Son of God: not only able to destroy the Temple of the living God but to conquer death given to one pierced in the flesh. Let our authority to come to the Father be by the body and blood of Jesus Christ. May the temple of God be our very soul; and when the flesh is pierced, the soul will be raised to new life by God's own Son.

Jesus began to weep. —John 11:35

Many see weeping as a sign of weakness; rather, weeping is a sign of strengthened faith; it shows that Christ has humbled our heart to the point of taking heart for others; it allows us to be strong for others. As we are reminded in Scripture: "As a father has compassion for his children, so the Lord has compassion for those who fear him" (Psalm 103:13). Christ's tender sympathy for these afflicted friends appeared by the troubles of His spirit. In all the afflictions of believers, He is afflicted; His concern for them was shown by the kind inquiry of His deceased friend. Being found in fashion as a man, He acts in the way and manner of the sons of men; His shedding of tears shows the true human character within Him. Tears of compassion resemble those of Christ. He sets us an example, that we may comfort the afflicted. "For we do not have a high priest who is unable to sympathize with our weaknesses, but we have one who in every respect has been tested as we are, yet without sin" (Hebrews 4:15). Yet we must take heart; these present afflictions are not to last forever. "He will wipe every tear from their eyes. Death will be no more" (Revelation 21:4). When He returns, the tears we shed will become for us tears of joy.

But you will receive power when the Holy Spirit has come upon you; and you will be my witnesses in Jerusalem, in all Judea and Samaria, and to the ends of the earth. —Acts 1:8

God desires to always be with His people. The Father sent the Son, and the Son, before His ascension, sent the Holy Spirit, that Christ's followers may be guided in the way they are to walk, thus being witnesses for Him both during and after His resurrection. Jesus had given His apostles instructions for the discharge of their duty, both before His death and since His resurrection, and this knowledge is enough for Christ's children. It is enough that Christ has given believers strength equal to their trials and services; that under the influence of the Holy Spirit they may, in one way or other, be witnesses for Christ on earth.

For now we see in a mirror, dimly, but then we will see face to face. Now I know only in part; then I will know fully, even as I have been fully known. —1 Corinthians 13:12

By the power of the Holy Spirit, Christ's love is shown in each of His children. The act of the Holy Spirit causes the spiritual growth of those same children. Paul explains this as witnessed through such gifts as speaking in tongues, prophesy, and knowledge. Such gifts show the presence of God's Spirit in our lives. These things help us to understand the sovereignty of our Lord, but in partiality, as if seeing a reflection in a mirror. Just as Paul proclaims: "O the depth of the riches and wisdom and knowledge of God! How unsearchable are his judgments and how inscrutable his ways! 'For who has known the mind of the Lord? Or who has been his counselor?'" (Romans 11:33-34). All things are dark and confused in this present world. This side of Heaven we will never know or comprehend the full wisdom, knowledge, and love of our Lord. The darkness of the sin of this world has hidden the face of God from us; we can only see but a mere glimpse of it. When God comes to live among us (Revelation 21:1-5), we will know Him fully as He knows us fully in this moment; our knowledge will be free from all obscurity and error. Christ is but mirrored here. May our lives tell His story—if only in reflection.

And because you are children, God has sent the Spirit of his Son into our hearts, crying, 'Abba! Father!' — Galatians 4:6

The Scriptures are filled with instances which God is addressed as "Father" and "Abba, Father." This is a childlike impulse to repeat the name of a loved one, the one who gave us life. Addressing God with the title "Father" reflects His love and care for us and encourages us to trust Him. Although by nature we are born the children of wrath and disobedience, we may become by grace children of love and partake of the nature of the children of God, for He will have all His children resemble Him. Among men the eldest son is heir; among the children of God, all share in the inheritance. May the temper and conduct of His children ever show our adoption, and may the Holy Spirit witness that we are children and heirs of God.

Chapter 9

Surrender

Indeed, your heavenly Father knows that you need all these things.
— **Matthew 6:32**

This truth reaches up and claims an eternal fact that each of God's created people can rest securely on: the fact that He is our heavenly Father. Once we can state this truth with full reassurance and faith, our soul will settle forever in the resting place of peace. It is not surprising that right after this statement, Jesus says, "But strive first for the kingdom of God and his righteousness" (vs. 33). We must come to God first, seeking His will, His way, and His kingdom.

The Spirit will purify our soul, and we will come to understand the circumstances in our life and confess, "Yes, Father, for such was your gracious will" (Matthew 11:26). We look at the back of God's work, trying to read the conclusions to each chapter He writes; we cannot read them, however, because He has not yet written them. God looks at the front of His work, taking each chapter one at a time, writing it out exactly the way it is meant to be; all the circumstances of our life fit perfectly together to form a beautiful narrative. Each of us will come to a finale of full understanding that everything God allows to happen in this life -good or bad- will take its proper place in God's great plan.

We were afflicted in every way—disputes without and fears within.
—2 Corinthians 7:5

Two very important lessons God means to teach us when He allows such strong and constant pressure upon us: He means to show us His all-sufficient strength and grace. This treasure in "clay jars, so that it may be made clear that this extraordinary power belongs to God and does not come from us" (2 Corinthians 4:7). God also means to bring us to a greater awareness of our dependence on Him; we are dependent on Him alone, and He is continually trying to show us that truth. We are held by His hands and reliant solely on Him.

Through the harsh difficulties, trials, and setbacks of life, we are better taught that we cannot stand on self-made strength, but we must rely on God

72

alone; and by His love and grace for us, He has given us Jesus Christ as our cornerstone to lean upon. Our stand must exhibit trust that would not dare to take even one step alone. The only way to learn faith is through countless trials. It is always better to learn to trust our Maker than to live a life of enjoyment without Him. Once faith is learned, it is an eternal treasure gained: an everlasting possession we hold. Without trust in God, and faith solely in our Lord Jesus Christ, even great riches will leave us in poverty. "We are afflicted in every way, but not crushed; perplexed, but not driven to despair; persecuted, but not forsaken; struck down, but not destroyed" (2 Corinthians 4:8-9).

He said, 'For now I know that you fear God, since you have not withheld your son, your only son, from me.' —Genesis 22:12

Abraham walked many years in faith with God and trusted Him completely, whatever the Lord may have asked of him or done to him. While his mind thought only of the things that seemed reasonable, fair, and just, Abraham's heart was gripped tightly to the Lord and His promises; his soul was unwavering for God's good pleasure, and his faith was "sharper than any two-edged sword" (Hebrews 4:12). Abraham feared the mighty power and majesty of the Lord. He feared the merciful grace of the Lord, and His promises kept time and time and time again. Abraham feared God in a way that set his eyes always on Him, and his ears listening to each word God spoke, desiring to fulfill His goodwill; nothing in Heaven or on earth could move him but God's voice.

Like Abraham, the longer we walk in faith with the Lord, the more we learn to trust Him, and the nearer our heart draws to our Heavenly Father. When we continue to see the works of the Lord, His plans carried out, and His promises kept, our soul becomes unwavering for His good pleasure. We too are able to say "Yes, my Lord." "The reward for humility and fear of the Lord is riches and honor and life" (Proverbs 22:4).

Woe to you who strive with your Maker, earthen vessels with the potter! Does the clay say to the one who fashions it, 'What are you making?' or 'Your work has no handles'?'

[And]

Thus says the Lord, the Holy One of Israel, and its Maker: Will you question me about my children, or command me concerning the work of my hands? —Isaiah 45:9&11

How common it is to hear God called to account for His dealings with humanity. We are but the mold for the potter's hands and shall be fashioned according to His pleasure. Countless times in Scripture we read of God proclaiming Himself as the one true God. Is this not a plausible title for our Maker? The one who shaped today surely has tomorrow in His view and will address it accordingly. It is simply labor enough to keep the events of today on track. Woe to the one who questions his maker and all that He does. Instead, let us turn these foolish questions and doubts into prayers and praise; instead of criticizing the one that shaped each star in the sky, let us shine forth our faith by trusting God, the one true God alone. "I know, O Lord that the way of human beings is not in their control, that mortals as they walk cannot direct their steps" (Jeremiah 10:23).

Commit your way to the Lord; trust in Him, and he will act.
— Psalm 37:5

To commit is to surrender; we must surrender our way -our life, desires, doubts, hopes, fears, and eventually our very soul- into the hands of Christ. Self-effort, when we try to take the battle into our own hands, hinders God's work. We must allow Him to work in our life. Pushing God to get the work done never finishes it but rather drives us to madness. Living stillness -stillness of the soul- is born of trust. Quiet tension is not 'trust', but just compressed anxiety. The only thing that will keep us from even the possibility of tension is to bring God in as the greatest factor in all that we do. God will act in our lives when we commit our ways to His care. We must do our duty, and then leave the event with God. The promise is very sweet: He shall bring that to pass, whatever it is, which we have committed to Him.

So do not worry about tomorrow, for tomorrow will bring worries of its own. Today's trouble is enough for today. —Matthew 6:34

Simply put: *let the unseen days be; today is more than enough.*[5] Do your duty faithfully now, and depend upon the mercy of God and His divine help for the troubles which are yet to come. God makes it clear: "I give you a day at a time; I opened your road for today to travel with Me. I cannot help you when you stumble, if your focus is on the morrow." Worry shows the weakness and folly of God's child; it wears us away. We are reminded to "not boast about tomorrow, for you do not know what a day may bring" (Proverbs 27:1). There is no assurance of tomorrow: if we will have one, or what it may bring; our worry is in vain. Trying to plan for tomorrow through worry, we stand still on our road for today. It is folly to increase the cares of today by borrowing worries from tomorrow. Worry will not control the future. By

---

[5]Tolkien, J.R.R., (August 12, 1988). *Unfinished Tales: The Lost Lore of Middle-earth Mass Market.* Del Rey publisher.

prayer and exercising of faith, we will gain strength to bear us up under our daily troubles; and arm us against the temptations that attend them. May none of these troubles and temptations move us, but the power of the Holy Spirit alone. We make full proof of our faith in God when we trust our self wholly to His disposal and surrender to the full authority of His guidance through the Spirit. Let us not try to see too far ahead that our eyes may miss the blessings of today; or try to hear God's voice in the morrow, when He speaks to our heart this day! We wait for tomorrow's sunrise…we do not realize today's has not yet set.

After crying out and convulsing him terribly, it came out. — Mark 9:26

Evil never surrenders its grasp without a tremendous fight. We always arrive at spiritual inheritance through the fierce conflicts of the battlefield. Each human being that wins spiritual freedom does so at the cost of bloodshed. Satan blocks our way, and the passage must be won through tears. When we are born-again in Christ, it is not in the open countryside but through the distress of the storm that we draw our strength. In the Acts of the Apostles, after strengthening many disciples for Christ, the eleven remaining apostles encouraged these ransomed disciples to continue in faith, saying to them: "It is through many persecutions that we must enter the kingdom of God" (Acts 14:22). Our Lord opened the way into His kingdom by facing many trials and enduring great pains, furthermore strengthening Himself to bear the burden of humanity's fall. We too must live life fully like our Lord; that our Heavenly Father may shape us as one of His own and bring us into His house forever.

And can any of you by worrying add a single hour to your span of life? — Matthew 6:27

Worry only heats the bearing, but never produces any steam, thus bringing one nowhere; many precious minutes are wasted. Worry becomes a hindrance. as it adds unnecessary friction to our lives. Friction caused by fretting shows the absence of God's grace in our lives. Clouding our heart and mind with worry, we show our lack of faith that God will take care of us. That is why we are continually reminded and encouraged to cast our care upon God (1 Peter 5:7), which is the only way to bring about lasting peace.

All this has happened to me! —Genesis 42:36

It is not uncommon to think that the world is against us. We are afflicted in body, estate, name, and in our relations; and we think all these things are against us when God is truly working them to be a weight of glory for us. In this way, our Lord conceals Himself and His favor; He rebukes and admonishes those for whom He has purposes of love. By sharp corrections and humbling convictions, He will break us of our sinful nature, humble the prideful heart, and bring our soul to true repentance. Yet before we can fully know Him or taste that He is gracious, He consults our good and sustains our soul to wait for Him. Our perseverance creates for us spiritual power; we must receive God's power and use it to rise above our circumstances. May we never yield to discouragement, determining to seek no other refuge; and humble ourselves more and more under our Lord's mighty hands. In due time He will answer our petitions and do for us more than we can expect.

> *But I do not count my life of any value to myself, if only I may finish my course and the ministry that I received from the Lord Jesus, to testify to the good news of God's grace.* —Acts 20:24

Wow! What a powerful truth for Paul to confess. At that point in his life, the only thing Paul was set on living for was to please his Heavenly Master. Living out His will, he saw himself only as a messenger for Christ. Paul knew that hardships and tribulations awaited him in Jerusalem, yet that did not keep him from moving forward to accomplish his mission for God. Much of his work for the Lord would be accomplished in Jerusalem after he had suffered many sorrows. To Paul, these were simply blessings of salvation from Heaven. The more he set his feet in the fires of suffering, the more they were washed with the blood of the Lamb. He could claim his victory always through Christ; the Lord became the center of Paul's life and work.

The course of our life turns but two ways: the way through the fires of tribulation or the sandy shores of a sunny beach. It is this first path that Paul chose to follow; and through the hardships he endured for Christ, the more the Lord was seen in his life. Tribulation's imprint is on every great accomplishment, and sufferings are the songs sung by the triumphant. We know that Christ has overcome this fallen world (John 16:33). We too overcome suffering and tribulation, if only we would learn to see Him through all of them. "Jesus said to them, 'My food is to do the will of him who sent me and to complete his work" (John 4:34).

> *He said, 'Naked I came from my mother's womb, and naked shall I return there; the Lord gave, and the Lord has taken away; blessed be the name of the Lord.'* —Job 1:21

All that Job had obtained was from the providence of God; Job humbled himself under the hand of God. He reasons from the common state of human life, which he describes in his suffering. But Job knows all is from God and determined by Him; the same idea Timothy reminds us in his first epistle: "we brought nothing into the world, so that we can take nothing out of it"

(1Timothy 6:7). Job looks above instruments and keeps his eye upon the first cause. Afflictions must not divert us from but quicken us to rejoicing in the Maker of all. If in all our troubles we look to the Lord, He will support us. The Lord is righteous. All we have is from Him; we have forfeited it by sin and ought not to complain if He takes any part, or all, from us.

Let us continually offer a sacrifice of praise to God. — Hebrews 13:15

There's an old song -Lifesong by Casting Crowns- that I often like to sing to myself. The truth of the refrain is what brings the most meaning to my life: *Let my lifesong sing to you*[6]

When we look at our life worth living, only to please our Lord and bring a smile to His face, hardships and setbacks do not seem worth fretting over; we start to see them simply as side notes to a beautiful story that God is writing. Our troubles and pains make no sense here; they seem to be added darkness in an already blackened world. But when God writes out our life to come, the past troubles will make splendid reading. Even in the times of hardships God never leaves His children, like a good parent who lets their child be exposed to a painful injury, not because they delight in seeing their child wounded, but because they want the child to never forget that "In life, we have painful falls, but I'm always here to pick you up." Let us always offer a sacrifice of praise to our Heavenly Father, making the refrain of our life song to bring a smile to God.

And after you have suffered for a little while, the God of all grace, who has called you to his eternal glory in Christ, will himself restore, support, strengthen, and establish you. —1Peter 5:10

To remain steadfast in our walk with God, we must pass the three stages of faith that grow stronger as we continue to walk in the love of the Lord. God desires to make us His own, but before that happens, we must have enough intellectual light to take the stand in a relationship with God. After coming to the knowledge of Christ, a small seed of faith is planted in our heart. It is our choice whether or not we desire this seed of faith to blossom into a beautiful flower. The Holy Spirit works together with our circumstances and setbacks, shaping our heart to find Christ. After choosing to be one with the Lord, we submit to this life of faith through the Holy Spirit. When we are baptized spiritually by the Holy Spirit, we sign the contract of faithfulness to Christ, being one with the Father. Once we have submitted to this relationship with God the Father through Christ, the testing will begin. Through the numerous trials, setbacks, and circumstances that we face, our

---

[6] Casting Crowns. (2018). *Lifesong*. https://castingcrowns.com/music/lifesong/

faith will be built stronger; Christ will begin to be ingrained in our hearts. The testing we go through that shapes our faith will cause us to see that Christ is our rock, our hope, and our redeemer. Through the testing of our faith, we will learn to lift our eyes to Christ, calling on Him in times of despair. We come to rely solely on Him.

Not one of us can be complete until we have been into the surge of the storm and have found the glorious fulfillment of the prayer, "Take me (as one of your own), make me (into the perfect image of your Son), break me (of my hard heart and love for the world)!" Once we have learned to lift our eyes toward Heaven, seeing Christ through our cloudy days, our faith will be forged with the fires of His Word and His promises. We will begin to see Christ not only in the trying moments but also during the times of rest. Our faith will begin to abide in us, so that through every circumstance in life (be it favorable or not), we see nothing but Christ. Our faith will become a wall of stone: not pierced, moved, or penetrated by any but God.

He said, 'Come.' So Peter got out of the boat, started walking on the water, and came toward Jesus. But when he noticed the strong wind, he became frightened, and beginning to sink, he cried out, 'Lord, save me!' —Matthew 14: 29-30

Who can forget the famous story of our Lord walking on the water? We too want to walk on the water with Christ; but the less we focus on Him, and the more we focus on the possibility of drowning beneath the threat of high winds and deep waters, we begin to sink under them, as Peter did when he saw the winds rushing up. Instead of fully focusing his attention solely on Christ, Peter turned and saw the threat of winds on the water, beginning to doubt his Lord's awesome power to help him rise above the waters. We too turn from Christ, looking instead at the headwinds of doubt and possible upcoming storms. We must, instead, focus fully on the Lord, who not only gives us the strength to rise above life's storms, but also helps us store up faith to steadily walk over them.

As we walk on the waters of life with our Lord, the winds of doubt and fear are crushed beneath the feet of our Savior, and the storms caused by wavy seas are calmed as we walk hand-in-hand with Christ. It is always better to weather the storms with Christ than to sail smooth seas without Him.

Cast all your anxiety on him, because he cares for you. —1 Peter 5:7

Anxiety arises from a lack of trust in God's providence. Satan's whole design is to devour and destroy the soul, and nothing comes easier than when we abandon God's love and care for us. We must leave every event in our lives and the lives of others to the wise and gracious disposal of God; this calms our spirit. Humility to cast our cares before Christ preserves peace in our heart and brings the soul to rest on firm ground. No difficulties will God's wisdom, power, and goodness not be able to conquer.

> *Which one of you, having a hundred sheep and losing one of them, does not leave the ninety-nine in the wilderness and go after the one that is lost until he finds it? When he has found it, he lays it on his shoulders and rejoices. And when he comes home, he calls together his friends and neighbors, saying to them, 'Rejoice with me, for I have found my sheep that was lost.' Just so, I tell you, there will be more joy in heaven over one sinner who repents than over ninety-nine righteous persons who need no repentance.* —Luke 15:4-7

The parable of the lost sheep shows the character of God and how dearly He loves His people. "Not wanting any to perish" (2 Peter 3:9), the Son of Man concentrates His thoughts, energy, and prayers on one soul among the herd of sheep who are thus gathered together. This parable is very applicable to God's assurance of man's redemption. The lost sheep is like sinners departed from God and exposed to certain ruin if not brought back to Him, yet they are not desirous to return.

Christ is earnest in bringing sinners home. That which is lost is one sheep, of small value compared with the rest, yet the Good Shepherd seeks diligently until He finds it. This emphasizes the various means and methods God makes use of to bring lost souls home to Himself, and the Savior's joy on their return to Him: "For the Son of Man came to seek out and to save the lost" (Luke 19:10). Sisters and brothers in Christ shall rejoice on that day, one-hundred-fold, knowing one more lost soul has been found for the sake of coming home to the Good Shepherd! How dearly, then, should we value the act of repentance, that leads us thus to salvation! "As he went ashore, he saw a great crowd; and he had compassion for them, because they were like sheep without a shepherd; and he began to teach them many things" (Mark 6:34).

> *Enter through the narrow gate; for the gate is wide and the road is easy that leads to destruction, and there are many who take it. For the gate is narrow and the road is hard that leads to life, and there are few who find it.* —Matthew 7:13-14

All people are either saints or sinners, godly or ungodly, born again in Christ or condemned to Satan. God offers us two choices: one is broad and wide, treading over level ground, a splendid and delightful walking path. The other -and much-rejected path- is narrow and hard, with scattered thorns of doubt and stones of difficulties blocking the path. Do we see the danger? There is obvious appeal to the wide gate and easy road. One may go in to this gate with all their lusts about them. It gives no check to appetites of passions and worldly love; it is a broad way. There are many paths in it; all are choices of sinful ways leading away from God. This is the gate of impenitence and unbelief, of carnal affections and fleshly lusts.

The narrow gate and hard road traveled leads to life, but one is not in Heaven as soon as they enter through this gate. This path must be walked through to its end which leads to the eternal life of the soul. To enter this gate, one must deny the luxuries of life and throw away what pleases the body. Self must be denied, and one's definition must lay in Christ alone. In the narrow gate, nothing is to be found that flatters the flesh, only that which brings joy to God, bringing the soul to peace. Christ is the narrow gate (John 10:7-9); opening this way, we are allowed to follow Him to heavenly heights.

Every tree that does not bear good fruit is cut down and thrown into the fire. —Matthew 7:19

Such fruit from the good tree is of the soul that roots itself deep in God's Word, not only hearing His words but living them to the full point of being like a tree that blossoms and grows strong, bearing many fruits, desiring as Christ does, that none shall perish. The fruitless tree is like the person that hears the Gospel call but chooses not to heed or act on its teachings, sowing no seeds of truth into the minds and hearts of men, and great will be his fall (Matthew 7:27) in the days of judgment. These are the trees that blossom but with poisonous berries, choking the ground on which the fruitful trees grow.

The one who spends a life apart from Christ "will suffer the punishment of eternal destruction, separated from the presence of the Lord and the glory of His might." (2 Thessalonians 1:9). Eternal separation from God will indeed be as a fire on which a dead tree is cast. Let us open our ears to gather Christ's good news, putting His teachings into action amongst a hurting world. May we be as a tree that bears good fruit for the Kingdom of Christ; may we confess with gladness, "As for me and my household, we will serve the Lord" (Joshua 24:15).

Yes, Father, for such was your gracious will. —Matthew 11:26

Like Jesus, we must trust God and His ways, knowing that the sovereign purpose and counsel of God is right. We must testify to the truth that His will and ways are the correct course, and praise Him for His wisdom and judgment. We confess the goodness of God by proclaiming His goodwill. The Father had delivered into Christ's hands all power, authority, and

80

judgment. We can be confident knowing that Christ works the will of the Father, not just for His kingdom but for the good of all His children.

My brothers and sisters, do you with your acts of favoritism really believe in our glorious Lord Jesus Christ? —James 2:1

What Christ teaches; James reminds us: to show favoritism is sinful. Such thoughts are opposed to the very lesson Christ teaches us: to "love your neighbor as yourself!" (Matthew 22:39). Those who are Christ's ought not to show or make such distinctions amongst His people by showing such judgment as to give favoritism and partiality between persons; "for God shows no partiality" (Romans 2:11).

We are Christ's alone who follow in His footsteps and strengthen our faith to perfectly reflect His image. Passing judgment by showing partiality and favoritism weakens the faith in our heart; we draw a barrier between God's people, which continues to the weakest of faith when we draw the same barrier between God's children. The Church becomes divided as it should not be. God's children must act as the one body of Christ. Showing such acts of favoritism, we become "judges with evil thoughts" (James 2:4); we base our final distinctions between people by what we can see only through the world's eyes. Let us leave the final judgment of each individual (including ourselves) in God's hands, as He is the rightful judge of all. And may we show no partiality but love all, as God loves us, "for they are all the work of his hands" (Job 34:19).

And free those who all their lives were held in slavery by the fear of death. —Hebrews 2:15

Many fear deaths, perhaps because they know not where they are headed in the afterlife. Paul makes it clear that Christ alone came as one of us so that He may die for the sins of His people. He alone is the one that holds "the keys of Death and Hades" (Revelation 1:18). By His resurrection, He has freed us from the damnation of dying to Satan. The firm faith in this truth is what will free the sinner from death. "For the law of the Spirit of life in Christ Jesus has set you free from the law of sin and of death" (Romans 8:2).

We mustn't fear what can kill the body, yet harm not the soul. The earthly body we are arrayed in is weak, but the soul that stands firm on the promise of redemption -that rests itself on the solid rock that is our God= are the ones that need not fear death, for there will be none, only life eternal with the Lord. Let us die, rather, to our sins: each, in turn, being crucified with Christ, thus becoming prisoners with Christ, knowing not the sinful nature we cast behind, nor the death that once waited at the door. One can only live peacefully when he is no longer a slave to the fear of death

> *Do not fear, you worm Jacob, you insect Israel!*
> *I will help you, says the Lord;*
> *your Redeemer is the Holy One of Israel.*
> *Now, I will make of you a threshing sledge,*
> *sharp, new, and having teeth;*
> *you shall thresh the mountains and crush them,*
> *and you shall make the hills like chaff.* —Isaiah 41:14-15

Nothing is more easily bruised or crushed than an insect; it is very delicate. A threshing tool can cut through rock and not be broken, leaving a mark upon the rock. The Almighty God can convert the two: He can take a nation or an individual with all the weakness of an insect and through His very spirit, He can endow that nation/individual with strength enough to leave their mark upon history. God can make us stronger than our circumstances and turn each situation to our good.

It is the worm: so little, so weak, so despised and trampled upon by everybody. God's people are as worms, in humble thoughts of themselves, and their enemies' haughty thoughts of them; worms, but not vipers, not of the serpent's seed. Every part of God's Word is calculated to humble man's pride and to make him appear little in his own eyes, insisting upon his need for God. Contrary to this weakness, the Lord will make all who call on His name to become a threshing instrument. God will make him fit for use, new, and having sharp spikes. This has fulfilment in the triumphs of the Gospel of Christ and all faithful followers of Christ over the power of darkness. Christ is building His kingdom with the broken, weakened, and failed things of this world: to lift life's biggest failure and take it to Heaven's heights! "A bruised reed he will not break, and a dimly burning wick he will not quench" (Isaiah 42:3).

> *No one can tame the tongue—a restless evil, full of deadly poison.*
> —James 3:8

-And-

> *But what comes out of the mouth proceeds from the heart, and this*
> *is what defiles.* —Matthew 15:18

From the tongue we bless and curse, speak truths and lies, slander our neighbor and love our brother.

The act of taming the tongue is not impossible, just extremely difficult. As James reminds us in verse 2 of Chapter 3: we all make many mistakes; not one of us is made holy but by the grace and love of the Lord. Our tongue is powerful, evil, and hurtful. Just as our deeds reveal our faith, our words reveal our heart. We cannot tame our tongue on our own because we can't change our sinful nature on our own. No one can tame the tongue without divine grace and assistance. This is just one of the ways Christ works in our lives; the longer we live by the divine grace of the Spirit, the firmer our heart is set on what is right, thus helping to change the words of our mouth: ready and willing to utter blessings to our Maker and our neighbors, crucifying the slander, lies, and curses that once came from the same lips, replacing them with blessings of thanksgiving, truths, and songs of praise. Let us speak out of the good treasure of our heart (Luke 6:45). Depending on this divine grace, let us take heed to bless and not curse; let us aim to be consistent in our words and actions, revealing our love for the Lord.

I know that you can do all things, and that no purpose of yours can be thwarted. 'Who is this that hides counsel without knowledge?' Therefore, I have uttered what I did not understand, things too wonderful for me, which I did not know. — Job 42:2-3

It usually takes a humbled heart to admit one's faults. Job was now aware of his guilt; he would no longer speak in his own excuse; he abhorred himself as a sinner in heart and life, especially for murmuring against God. By the teachings of men, God reveals His Son to us; but by the teachings of His Spirit, He reveals His Son *in* us (Galatians 1:16) and changes us into the same image (2 Corinthians 3:18). It concerns us to be deeply humbled for the sins of which we are convinced. Self-loathing is ever the companion of true repentance. The Lord will bring those whom He loves to adore Him in self-abasement, while true grace will always lead us to confess our sins without self-justification.

Then everyone who calls on the name of the Lord shall be saved; for in Mount Zion and in Jerusalem there shall be those who escape, as the Lord has said, and among the survivors shall be those whom the Lord calls. —Joel 2:32

The first church of God was founded on mount Zion: the place where King Solomon built the first temple of the Lord and established the worship to the Lord. This was called the place of the Lord: the very place where God was worshipped. Servants shall call upon the name of the Master and will be delivered: delivered from the cruel judgment of God's wrath poured out upon those who are idol to their sin and delivered from an eternity away from our heavenly Maker. These ones alone, who call upon the Name of the Lord, who seek to know Him, follow Him, and put faith solely in Him, who turn from self to Christ and from carnal desires to spiritual longings, who worship and have obedience to the Lord as He is, and depend upon His whole being, the self-same, will be saved.

By His grace, God must first call us to Himself, and He does. We in turn, obeying the call to come near call upon His Name, further bringing glory to God and deliverance upon ourselves. Similar words are spoken by Paul to the Romans, yet painted with a clearer picture of what it is like to come to the Lord: "if you confess with your lips that Jesus is Lord and believe in your heart that God raised him from the dead, you will be saved" (Romans 10:9).

Paul gives us a two-fold responsibility: we must devote and give up to God our soul and our body: our soul in believing with the heart (paving the way to righteousness) and our body in confessing with the mouth. Of such faith, no sinner shall be ashamed before God, and he ought to glory in it before men.

For he wounds, but he binds up; he strikes, but his hands heal. — Job 5:18

Calm follows after the destruction of the storm! God's usual method is first to wound and then to heal, first to convince and then to comfort, first to humble and then to exalt. A good man is happy though he is afflicted, for he has not lost his enjoyment of God, nor his title to Heaven. He is happy *because* he is afflicted; correction mortifies his corruptions, weans his heart from the world, draws him nearer to God, brings him to his Bible, and brings him to his knees. The proud are brought low by the wounds of humility. Though God wounds, yet He supports His people under afflictions and in due time delivers them. Making a wound is often part of the cure.

I will say to God, Do not condemn me; let me know why you contend against me. —Job 10:2

As if complaining to God may change our mind, we continually ask Him- "Why?" Complaint seems to comfort, but it further condemns. God means to contend with us; contending with His children, God always has a reason for it. He is never angry without a cause; our ill-natured reaction to God's righteousness leads us to complaint when hardships strive against us. Faith and patience would keep us from becoming weary of our life and hating it. Being weary of God -who gives vent to our soul by violent wounds- the bitterness of our soul speaks out against us.

Being left alone by Satan is *not* evidence of blessing! The darker circumstances get and the harder to bear trials become, the stronger our faith will grow to let go of our self and rely on God alone. He means to bless His children, that through hardships, we may learn to see Him more clearly through all things; that He alone may be our light in the dark places. God never promised an easy road, only a safe landing point!

> *At that moment the cock crowed for the second time. Then Peter remembered that Jesus had said to him, 'Before the cock crows twice, you will deny me three times.' And he broke down and wept.*
> —Mark 14:72

It is easy coming to the truth proclaiming, as Peter did, "Even though all become deserters, I will not" (Mark 14:29). But we must take heed, lest we fall into temptation. The spirit is willing, but the body is weak, even of the one who walked in faith three years with the Lord. The most faithful of Christ's followers may at times turn against Him; and when the truth of our sinfulness comes fully to mind, our heart is broken and humbled; we know nothing but to weep in remorse and bitterness because of our fault. Let us not stand forever in our sinfulness, but by His love and grace. Return to the Lord with weeping and supplication, seeking forgiveness, and to be raised up by the Holy Spirit.

Chapter 10

Testing the Heart

Do not store up for yourselves treasures on earth, where moth and rust consume and where thieves break in and steal; but store up for yourselves treasures in heaven, where neither moth nor rust consumes and where thieves do not break in and steal. For where your treasure is, there your heart will be also. — **Matthew 6:19-21**

Jesus tells His followers that earthly treasures will not last: we cannot take them to Heaven when we are called home; and when we come home to be with our Maker, earthly riches will be forgotten. God desires the whole heart; He will not share it with the world. We can only serve one master; we must love God and deny the world, or love this world and deny God.

Worldliness is a common and fatal symptom of hypocrisy; by no sin can Satan have a surer hold of the soul than one that sinks under the desires of this world. Isaiah illustrates this very lust when he speaks of the king of Babylon (Isaiah 14:12). His soul was cast from Heaven, as it belonged not to God but this world; he set it upon worldly gain. Given the name Lucifer, the Babylonian king metaphorically symbolized the outshining of all the kings of the earth by his great splendor. So, it is with those who "store up treasures for themselves but are not rich toward God" (Luke 12:21); their soul is set upon sinking sand.

Christ counsels us to make our best desires the joys and glories of the other world, those things not seen which are eternal, and to place our happiness in them. There are treasures in Heaven that will be awaiting the child of God. It is our wisdom to give all diligence to make our title of eternal life sure through Jesus Christ, to look on all things here below as not worthy to be compared with it, and to be content with nothing short of it. It is happiness above and beyond the changes and chances of time: an inheritance incorruptible.

But strive for the greater gifts. And I will show you a still more excellent way. —1 Corinthians 12:31

Humanity thirsts for pleasure merely in the carnal desires that satisfy the flesh. Like the fleshly body -wasting away, slowly decaying to become nothing- the gifts most often longed for are the ones that satisfy but for a time. But I say, "Live by the Spirit" (Galatians 5:16). Unlike these carnal gifts that satisfy the flesh, the greater gifts are the ones only God can give: the gifts that cannot die away and needn't be replaced. The gifts God gives satisfy the soul. God seeks to give spiritual gifts, ones longed after by the heart, and the soul thirsts for. In seeking and grasping these greater gifts from our Maker, faith is strengthened with a never-ending stream of God's blessings, and the soul is content to rest on none other than the One that satisfies it.

This more excellent way that Christ means to teach us is the way of life, with Him as our leader grasping our hand, guiding our heart, and showing us the road to the Father. This more excellent way -this *most excellent* way- is the way wrought in the soul that is saved, the one that comes to Christ, seeking for blessings that save, blessings that needn't be replaced or dissatisfy the seeker—the gifts that cannot be made or given by human hands, but only by God. May we yearn for the spiritual gifts, grasping them from our Maker and holding them forever in our soul.

Beloved, never avenge yourselves, but leave room for the wrath of God; for it is written, 'Vengeance is mine, I will repay, says the Lord.' —Romans 12:19

Instead of responding to our enemy on account of injustice, we should respond with voiceless, confident calmness; responding in this way, rather than taking vengeance, shows a deep display of Christ's character in us. It takes a very mature child of God to express this type of response to injustice. Many times in Scripture, Jesus shows us how He handled injustice. He went off by Himself many times to be alone with the Father (See Matthew 15:29 and Mark 6:32). There were also times when Jesus wept (See John 11:35 and Luke 19:41). We often think of weeping as a sign of weakness; but weeping shows the strength, calmness, and quiet of the soul, responding with tears instead of wrath. The Lord is our avenger; He will repay injustice in His good timing. All that matters is our loyalty to Christ.

The wicked are not so, but are like chaff that the wind drives away. Therefore, the wicked will not stand in the judgment, nor sinners in the congregation of the righteous; for the Lord watches over the way of the righteous, but the way of the wicked will perish. —Psalm 1:4-6

-And-

Therefore they shall be like the morning mist or like the dew that goes away early, like chaff that swirls from the threshing floor or like smoke from a window. —Hosea 13:3

The psalmist draws a fine line between the righteous and the wicked. The righteous are those who seek after the way of wisdom, desiring to honor God and His rightful will, as opposed to the wicked who are ungodly and walk in the way of sinners to the seat of the scornful; they have no delight in the law of God; the fruit the wicked bring forth is only that which is evil. Wheat is separated from the chaff at threshing time; the former is stored in barns; the latter is thrown out as it is useless, fruitless, and dead. Such are the ways of the wicked, who "will not stand in the judgment" (Psalm 1:5). Chaff has no firm ground on which to flourish, no root or moisture; nothing in it that is solid and substantial to the soul.

The wicked are destitute of all that is good; they are without the knowledge of the Father or faith in Christ and love for Him, not knowing of His grace and fruitfulness, having not the glory of the Spirit. The righteous flourish, planting seeds of faith in wandering souls, producing the fruit of love, faithfulness, and grace; like a fruitful tree, the righteous give much satisfaction to the one who gathers its fruit. May we choose the way of the righteous, laboring to plant seeds of love and grace, desiring to bear much fruit. And when the One comes to separate the wheat from the chaff, may we not be found amongst the chaff, driven away with the dust on the threshing floor.

But his master replied, 'You wicked and lazy slave! You knew, did you, that I reap where I did not sow, and gather where I did not scatter? Then you ought to have invested my money with the bankers, and on my return, I would have received what was my own with interest. So, take the talent from him, and give it to the one with the ten talents. For to all those who have, more will be given, and they will have an abundance; but from those who have nothing, even what they have will be taken away. As for this worthless slave, throw him into the outer darkness, where there will be weeping and gnashing of teeth.' —Matthew 25:26-30

A similar parable is found in the 19th chapter of Luke. God has given each of His created people a wide variety of gifts, and He expects us to employ those gifts in His service. It is not acceptable merely to put those gifts on a closet shelf and ignore them. Like the three servants, we do not have gifts of the same degree; the return God expects of us is commensurate with the gifts we have been given.

The servant who received one talent was condemned because he did nothing with what he was given. The gifts we receive from God include skills, abilities, family connections, social positions, education, experiences, and so much more. We are to use whatever we have been given for God's purposes. The severe consequences to the unproductive servant, far beyond anything triggered by mere business mediocrity, tells us that we are to invest our life, not waste it; to the one who has been given much, using it for the sole good of God's glory, to him will be given more gifts, thus to be used further for the glory of God.

Above all else, guard your heart, for everything you do flows from it. —Proverbs 4:23

See here the very words of God portrayed throughout the entirety of this chapter. Above all instruction, one is to guard the heart and take extra precaution to what is stored therein: as the heart feeds the soul, and the soul thrives on the things wrought in the heart, it is the place of all spiritual wisdom, and the storehouse of all that is desired in this life.

If the heart is quickened and sanctified by the grace of God, one will live a life of faith and holiness here and enjoy everlasting life hereafter. If the heart is right, so will the actions be. They are regulated and denominated by it, and will then spring forth from right principles and be directed to right ends, with right views on what to be performed. Great care, therefore, should be taken of the heart, since so much depends upon it, and it is so well known to God, the searcher of it. "The good person out of the good treasure of his heart produces good, and the evil person out of his evil treasure produces evil, for out of the abundance of the heart his mouth speaks" (Luke 6:45).

May we seek the purification of the Spirit, making the heart the home of all that is spiritually right, acting upon those things which bring glory to God and set the example of His love. As is one's heart is, such is his state now, and will be hereafter.

Why, O Lord, do you stand far off? Why do you hide yourself in times of trouble? —Psalm 10:1

In direct contrast to the preceding psalm, David seems to point to the present condition of the world in which the wicked seem to triumph over the righteous. However, a cry unto God to act seems remote, to not be heard; He seems to be disinterested. God might seem disinterested when we walk by sight rather than by faith, when physical observations overrule the spiritual facts of the Divine.

Walking by sight, not by faith, causes us to stumble: our "amen" is continually replaced with the lament of "why?" Continuing to ask God "why" leads to frustration, impatience, and despair; it seems that God is hiding from us. We need never forget that God remains near to His children. We must "walk by faith, not by sight" (2 Corinthians 5:7). When our mind and heart are rooted deeply in God's love, grace, and mercy, we walk according to His will: by the guidance of the Holy Spirit, not by the everyday physical presence we see surrounding us. David shifts his focus to the Divine (vs. 12-18). May we also shift our sight, focusing on God's divine truths.

> *Whoever walks with the wise becomes wise, but the companion of fools suffers harm.* —Proverbs 13:20

Those that fear the Lord as an act of bringing Him glory are accounted wise among men. They let the presence of the Holy Spirit abide deeply within their hearts, showing them in which way they are to walk: walking that road with confidence, knowing the Lord is ever-present. The fool is the one that delights in not understanding, taking pleasure in pursuing the wrong things: scoffing at living in wisdom. "Fools despise wisdom and instruction" (Proverbs 1:7). Taking up with such foolishness, our own faith that the Lord has wrought in us will be hindered, leading to further destruction of our soul. Our Lord desires that we learn from those that fear Him and keep His commands, thus, in turn, obtaining further wisdom. Our Lord does not ask us to stop evangelizing to the lost, to look away from the foolish; He asks still that we would be His witnesses to all people: the foolish as well as the wise. In such a way, the foolish may be led to the paths of the wise, learning to fear the Lord, keep His commands, and live by the guidance of the Holy Spirit.

> *Take my instruction instead of silver, and knowledge rather than choice gold, for wisdom is better than jewels, and all that you may desire cannot compare with her.* —Proverbs 8:10-11

As the saying goes, *All that is gold does not glitter.*[7] One cannot count on gold in times of trouble; silver is but useless in one's hand when the storms of life hit. These treasures are beautiful on the outside, glimmering brighter than the stars of Heaven; but there is no lasting value, no inner beauty. Let us look to the inner beauty of the heart, desiring, the wisdom of God, the instruction and guidance that comes to us from the Spirit, and the strength we find only through the resurrection of our Lord Jesus Christ.

---

[7] Tolkein, JRR, (1997) *The Lord of the Rings.* (2nd ed., pp.241). Houghton Mifflin Company

May we grasp this truth and hold it close to our souls: those things wrought of the Spirit -things that are of eternal value are of much more worth and satisfaction than what lingers here on earth, be it gold, silver, or precious gems. Let us count the wisdom and knowledge of God more precious than these glimmering treasures. James reminds us how good God is at blessing us with wisdom if we but ask for it with a sincere heart (James 1:5). Let us count the wisdom, knowledge, and instruction that comes only from our Maker and hold it above the value of the gold and silver we find here. May our soul glimmer bright like rubies but with the knowledge of God; and may it shine with the clear image of Christ. "Keep hold of instruction; do not let go; guard her, for she is your life" (Proverbs 4:13).

Set your minds on things that are above, not on things that are on earth. —Colossians 3:2

Unless one's affections are set on Heavenly blessings, they will never be sought after properly. As Heaven and earth contradict one another, both cannot be followed together; and affection to the one will weaken and abate affection to the other. To be dead to sin, then, is to die to carnal desires and longings, to extinguish within our heart and mind that which brings us gain, and despise earthly things. We set in its place, rather, the spiritual blessings that we shall receive from Christ's hands. Our affections shall be set upon the heavenly world where the true treasure lies, and look above this temporal one.

Rejoice in hope, be patient in suffering, persevere in prayer. — Romans 12:12

Paul states it clearly and relates these three actions together as one persistent method for us to follow.

Rejoice in hope: there's always a reason to have hope. When we always look to the Lord, we are refreshed each day with the hope we have in Christ, the Guardian of our days, and Redeemer of our soul.

Be patient in suffering: God calls us often to exercise our faith by triumphing over our setbacks; the most diligent, Christ-like way to show such patience and faith is to wait quietly while God works in our lives. Questioning Him never brings us out of suffering; it only drives the thorns deeper. Patience for God's sake is true piety. Those that rejoice in hope are likely to be patient in tribulation.

And persist in prayer: we must stay strong in our prayer lives; never becoming weary of it. Taking part in the sorrows and joys of our brothers and sisters will uplift the Church and strengthen each of us in turn, bringing our soul closer to Heaven.

> *Beloved, do not be surprised at the fiery ordeal that is taking place among you to test you, as though something strange were happening to you. But rejoice insofar as you are sharing Christ's sufferings, so that you may also be glad and shout for joy when his glory is revealed.* —1 Peter 4:12-13

Crucifixion comes before coronation; burning must come before the growth; the joy for the tear, the peace for the pain. We must be crucified with Christ if we are to share in His joy. We must suffer in the flesh, (1 Peter 4:1) if we are to rid ourselves of sin: no longer desiring to live for earthly gain, but solely for the will of God.

Brothers and sisters, be not surprised when circumstances heat the fires hotter! Rejoice, knowing that Christ walks with us in the flames: "a very present help" (Psalm 46:1) to those who call on His name. Paul reminds us: "we suffer with him so that we may also be glorified with him" (Romans 8:17).

> *How the Lord in his anger has humiliated daughter Zion!*
> *He has thrown down from heaven to earth*
> *the splendor of Israel;*
> *he has not remembered his footstool in the day of his anger.*
> —Lamentations 2:1

Sin is the source and cause of our miseries. We are susceptible to God's wrath and judgment when sin is set in the way of repentance. God will bring us down to true humility: to the point of relying on nothing and no one but Him, so that in our humility, we may realize that He is the only source of true happiness and joy.

God is not an enemy to His people when He is angry with them and corrects them, or when He withdraws His protection. It is just with God to cast down by judgment those who debase themselves by sin. It becomes necessary, though painful, to turn the thoughts of the afflicted to the hands of God lifted against them.

When we cast away our pride caused by the calamities of our sinfulness and cast ourselves down to the point of true humility and need, then God withdraws His hands of wrath and judgment. God's wrath lies against our sins and iniquities, not against us alone. True humility shows us our need, and God is ready to provide for our needs if we would only put an end to pride and humble our hearts to the point of reliance solely on Him. "For you deliver a humble people, but the haughty eyes you bring down" (Psalm 18:27).

To the pure all things are pure, but to the corrupt and unbelieving nothing is pure. Their very minds and consciences are corrupted.
—Titus 1:15

Paul talks about the purity of one's soul. In the Old Testament, the act of physical washing was an act of purification. When the debt of humanity's sin was paid in full through the body and blood of Christ, the act of purification came through believing in and acceptance of God's Son. We are justified from all sin only by Christ's righteousness and are clean through the Word of absolution spoken by Him. Sprinkled upon the conscience is the cleansing of all sin through the blood of Christ by which we are purged and cleansed.

The clean water of sanctifying grace is upon those who are purified. A clean heart and spirit are created within them, cleansed by faith, and principles of grace and holiness are formed, graces that are genuine and true, and faith unfeigned. Hope is not hypocritical, and love is without concealment. In response to all this, one will spiritually cleanse his soul from the destruction of sin and pollution of iniquity.

"Finally, beloved, whatever is true, whatever is honorable, whatever is just, whatever is pure, whatever is pleasing, whatever is commendable, if there is any excellence and if there is anything worthy of praise, think about these things" (Philippians 4:8).

For all who exalt themselves will be humbled, and those who humble themselves will be exalted. —Luke 14:11

There is a sharp contrast between selfishness and selflessness: choosing to exalt self and one's own cares above the needs of others; or choosing to think more often of God's people, reaching a loving hand out in kindness to help the poor and afflicted, putting our own life and cares on the back-burner.

Christ reveals this truth in showing that works of charity are better than works of show. A man's pride will bring him low; and before true honor will come true humility. Christ goes on to tell us that "you will be blessed, because they cannot repay you, for you will be repaid at the resurrection of the righteous" (vs. 24). Do not look for future honor, but know that our Father in Heaven reads the minds and hearts of men, and He will honor the humble-hearted in due time.

We do not dare to classify or compare ourselves with some of those who commend themselves. But when they measure themselves by one another, and compare themselves with one another, they do not show good sense. We, however, will not boast beyond limits, but will keep within the field that God has assigned to us, to reach out even as far as you. — 2 Corinthians 10:12-13

The early followers of Christ had a deep sense of pride, selfishness, and flattery. They made themselves the standard of excellence and judged everyone and everything by that standard. How unwise and foolish self-complacency is! Paul fixes a good rule for this conduct; namely, not to boast of things without his measure, which was the measure God had distributed to him. There is not a more fruitful source of error than the judging of people and/or opinions by our own prejudices. How common it is for persons to judge their own spiritual character by the opinions and maxims of the world around them! And of all flattery, self-flattery is the worst. But how different are the rules of God's world! Therefore, instead of praising ourselves, we should strive to prove ourselves to God; and by seeking His approval, our heart will be made humble. Let us take glory in the Lord of our salvation, and in all other things only as evidence of His love or means of promoting His glory. Instead of praising ourselves or seeking the praise of men, let us desire that honor which comes from God, through Christ alone.

Therefore, to keep me from being too elated, a thorn was given me in the flesh, a messenger of Satan to torment me, to keep me from being too elated. — 2 Corinthians 12:7

The apostle gives an account of the method God took to keep him humble and to prevent his being lifted up above measure, on account of the visions and revelations he had. We are not told what this thorn in the flesh was - whether some great trouble or some great temptation-, but God often brings this good out of the evil that the reproaches of our enemies help to hide pride from us. If God loves us, He will keep us from being exalted above measure; thus, spiritual burdens are ordered to cure spiritual pride. This thorn in the flesh is said to be a messenger of Satan which he sent for evil, but God used it for his good.

See, I have refined you, but not like silver; I have tested you in the furnace of adversity. —Isaiah 48:10

Freedom from suffering leads to uselessness. We should welcome the opportunity to be refined, to be tested. "But he disciplines us for our good, in order that we may share his holiness" (Hebrews 12:10). Just as Silver is refined and shaped by fire, likewise, all of God's children must go through the heated furnace of afflictions and troubles, trials and pain, that shapes their hearts and sets their souls to rest solely in Christ. One cannot call himself

94

God's true child until his faith has felt the heat of this furnace, and his eyes see none but Christ in the flames.

Many are the afflictions of the righteous, but God delivers them out of it all. It may be a long while ere deliverance comes, but for us in the light of Christ, death has no sting (1 Corinthians 15:55). Affliction is instead a blessing: it releases us from our fallen state and sinfulness and ushers us back into perfection. God has a furnace of affliction for us all to go through in this life that He might prepare us for entry into perfection with Him. "Blessed is anyone who endures temptation. Such a one has stood the test and will receive the crown of life that the Lord has promised to those who love him" (James 1:12).

The mouths of the righteous utter wisdom, and their tongues speak justice. —Psalm 9:4

-And-

For you have maintained my just cause; you have sat on the throne giving righteous judgment. —Psalm 37:30

The Lord loves justice. By His grace and guidance from the Holy Spirit, He directs the thoughts, affections, and designs of His children. By His providence, He overrules events, to make their way plain.

"But the upright enjoy God's favor" (Proverbs 14:9). The righteous seek to follow such paths that the Lord lays, seeking after wisdom and justice and learning of the divine character of God. This wisdom and justice David speaks of is from the divine nature of God; it reveals His character. The righteous who walks in the ways of the Almighty utter such truths of wisdom and justice toward their neighbors, further reflecting the character of God present in their lives. When such justice is shown, "it is a joy to the righteous, but dismay to evildoers" (Proverbs 21:15).

Where is the one who is wise? Where is the scribe? Where is the debater of this age? Has not God made foolish the wisdom of the world? For since, in the wisdom of God, the world did not know God through wisdom, God decided, through the foolishness of our proclamation, to save those who believe. For Jews demand signs and Greeks desire wisdom. —1 Corinthians 1:20-22

Similar words are spoken in Isaiah 33:18; however, the meaning is quite different. Isaiah speaks with the authority of God, addressing the Jews after their captivity in Assyria. Paul speaks to his readers of the power and wisdom of Christ.

The preaching of salvation for lost sinners by the sufferings and death of the Son of God, if explained and faithfully applied, appears foolishness to those in the way of destruction; the sensual, the covetous, the proud and ambitious alike see that the Gospel opposes their favorite pursuits. But those who receive the Gospel, and are enlightened by the Spirit of God see more of God's wisdom and power in the doctrine of Christ crucified than in all His other works. God left a great part of the world to follow the dictates of man's boasted reason, and the event has shown that human wisdom is folly and is unable to find or retain the knowledge of God as the Creator. By the foolishness of preaching, the one who believes will be saved. The thing preached is foolishness to worldly-wise people; the Gospel ever was and ever will be foolishness to all on the road to destruction.

Christ is the power and wisdom of the living God. "For it is written, 'I will destroy the wisdom of the wise, and the discernment of the discerning I will thwart'" (Vs. 19). So, let us not boast of our own moral wisdom, but let us always remember that the source of our strength and wisdom comes only through the person of Jesus Christ.

> *But God chose what is foolish in the world to shame the wise; God chose what is weak in the world to shame the strong; God chose what is low and despised in the world, things that are not, to reduce to nothing things that are, so that no one might boast in the presence of God.* —1 Corinthians 1:27-29

-And-

> *Thus says the Lord: Do not let the wise boast in their wisdom, do not let the mighty boast in their might, do not let the wealthy boast in their wealth; but let those who boast boast in this, that they understand and know me, that I am the Lord; I act with steadfast love, justice, and righteousness in the earth, for in these things I delight, says the Lord.* — Jeremiah 9:23-24

It is not what man has done that all flesh may glory, but rather it is in the all-sufficient grace and salvation of God. We have no right to call ourselves righteous but for the body and blood of our Savior. No one may boast of being high elect and keeping with the law but by the sacrifice and resurrection of our Lord. The selfish ambition man puts on the elect things of this world God brings to the lowest point of shame, implying the reliance one must depend upon that comes only from the Lord. In this way, God brings humanity to the point of knowing full reliance on Him; that no one may boast in themself. Wisdom shall come only by the preaching and keeping of the Gospel, and strength through the person and works of Jesus Christ.

Deep calls to deep
at the thunder of your cataracts;
all your waves and your billows
have gone over me. —Psalm 42:7

Comparable to the deep waters of the sea, our struggles, trials, and temptations can be closely related to the very deep of God's waters. These came pouring down, one after another, upon the psalmist. As soon as one affliction ended, another came, as one calling to another, and were clamorous, troublesome, and very grievous and distressing. These afflictions David refers to as God's waves and God's billows; just like waves on the sea. They are appointed and sent by God; in like manner, they can also be overruled by God and made to work for the good of His children, if we but keep our faith strong and our prayer life consistent, focusing not on the overwhelming rage of our trials, that seem at times as fierce as a storm on the sea, but rather on the One who calms the seas, calming the storms in our life.

The way to forget our miseries (the storms of life) is to remember the God of our mercies. If one trouble follows hard after another, if all seem to combine for our ruin, let us remember they are all appointed and overruled by the Lord. The deep faith wrought in our soul overrules the depths of the stormy seas.

For where there is envy and selfish ambition, there will also be disorder and wickedness of every kind. — James 3:16

James speaks of two very different kinds of wisdom: one such as the world can give, and that wisdom which comes only from above. Envy is born of selfish ambition which arises when we are counseled to follow such wisdom as the world gives. This wisdom is set on the theme of being successful and having such a life: namely, getting the most of what we want of life. Such thoughts persuade us to covert what belong to others, giving birth to envy, lies, lusts, deceit, and the like. This wisdom runs on the fuel of selfishness and self-serving ambition. In the previous verses, James made clear that such so-called wisdom is *not* God's wisdom. Let us seek the wisdom that comes only from God by the grace of the Spirit, asking of it from God (James 1:5). In place of envy, there is brotherly love; in place of lies, there is truth spoken; and where there is selfishness, may there be selflessness and self-sacrificing for the needs of our neighbors and fellow brothers and sisters in Christ.

And this is the testimony: God gave us eternal life, and this life is in his Son. Whoever has the Son has life; whoever does not have the Son of God does not have life. — 1 John 5:11-12

Eternal life is the central theme to the changed state of the believer: confidence and surety of salvation only through the blood of God's own Son. The surety in the faith of this salvation humbles, heals, and comforts the soul of which has no other ground to rest itself secure.

The only way to eternal life is the overcoming of sin and victory gained in this world: the central subject to this last chapter of John's epistle focuses on Christ and the overcoming of sin which we achieve through Him; furthermore, the firm faith held by the believer is that victory gained. He that refuses to trust and honor Christ as the Son of God, who disdains to submit to His teaching, to rely on His atonement and intercession, or to obey Him, is dead in sin; there is no victory won, only death unheeded. He alone that conquers the world is the one who *knows* that Jesus is the Son of God (vs. 5).

> *But Jesus said, 'Someone touched me; for I noticed that power had gone out from me.' When the woman saw that she could not remain hidden, she came trembling; and falling down before him, she declared in the presence of all the people why she had touched him, and how she had been immediately healed. He said to her, 'Daughter, your faith has made you well; go in peace.'* — Luke 8:46-48

It is like that with God's children: when we touch the heart of Christ with our faithfulness, His power comes to us to strengthen and heal, bringing us peace. Christ's love, grace, peace, mercy, and strength is sufficient, not only for Him to give but for us to grasp. His power is strong enough to heal, if only we would reach out and touch His heart with our faithfulness.

> *In the same way, you who are younger must accept the authority of the elders. And all of you must clothe yourselves with humility in your dealings with one another, for 'God opposes the proud, but gives grace to the humble.' Humble yourselves therefore under the mighty hand of God, so that he may exalt you in due time.* — I Peter 5:5-6

Humility preserves peace and order in all Christian churches and societies; pride disturbs them. Where God gives the grace to be humble, He will give wisdom, faith, and holiness. To be humble and be subject to God will bring greater comfort to the soul than the gratification of pride and ambition; but it is to be in due time, not in the timing that seems fair or good to us, but God's own wisely appointed time. What difficulties will not the firm belief of His wisdom, power, and goodness overcome? Be humble under His hand. A firm belief that the divine will and counsels are right, calms the spirit of the distraught individual.

And as he sowed, some seeds fell on the path, and the birds came and ate them up. Other seeds fell on rocky ground, where they did not have much soil, and they sprang up quickly, since they had no depth of soil. But when the sun rose, they were scorched; and since they had no root, they withered away. Other seeds fell among thorns, and the thorns grew up and choked them. Other seeds fell on good soil and brought forth grain, some a hundredfold, some sixty, some thirty. — Matthew 13:4-8

Which seed sown do you wish to be? Do you care merely to read through Scripture, not wishing to understand what Christ teaches? Like a bad student, you care not to listen to and understand the Great Teacher. This is the one whose heart sits still, and the seed finds no soil to plant itself in. Do you hear Christ's teachings and accept them, as is common to man to accept a message of joy? But not knowing that temptations lie ahead, you are struck down by the heaviness of doubt and despair. The rocks of sorrow, fear, and doubt crush your seed into many pieces.

Is it more profitable to let the lies, lusts, and temptations of a sinful world choke your heart? A choked seed, (overcome by thorns), is a useless seed. Or do you wish to root the seed sown in your heart deep in the Word of God, taking the promises of the Lord and storing them deep in your heart? Putting His Word to use, your heart is rooted deeply in the firm soil of Christ's love; choosing to root it there, you bear fruit for God's kingdom on earth; as more hearts take this fruit from you, sharing in the richness of its blessings, the kingdom of God is strengthened and expanded. Where do you wish to plant the seed sown in your heart?

But we had hoped that he was the one to redeem Israel. Yes, and besides all this, it is now the third day since these things took place. — Luke 24:21

The two apostles walking by Jesus' side had given up all hope. They walked by Jesus' side, declaring their shattered faith that He would come again. On the road to Emmaus, Jesus had to remind these men yet again of what He had told them: that He would be raised in three days. Jesus had to declare to them "how foolish you are, and how slow of heart to believe" (vs. 25). Instead of relying on Christ, they relied only on what their eyes did not see; if they had looked with deeper faith, they would have seen that Christ was the one who walked at their side.

Are we not in danger of having these very words said to us? We can afford to lose every possession we have except our faith in God, the God of truth and love. Letting our hope dwindle on the edges of shattered dreams, our hope also is lost. How foolish we become not to believe, and not to take God at His word.

May our faith always be in the present tense; that we will *have* hope, not that our faith will linger upon what we cannot see, but that it may rest secured on the promises God reveals to us. God's love doubles in the storms of life, strengthening our faith and increasing our hope. May we always *have hope,* knowing that Christ walks by our side.

Chapter 11

Adoration

Come and see what God has done: he is awesome in his deeds among mortals. He turned the sea into dry land; they passed through the river on foot. There we rejoiced in him. —**Psalm 66:5-6**

Many times God leads us into the net but to show His mighty power and works, just to lead us out again (See vs. 11-12). At these moments we are often found blaming, cursing, and questioning God for our ill fate. We do not see the plans He has for us to prosper, leading us out of our nets by another way that is not in league with our plans or our timing. Ideally, we are left praising the Lord for His almighty works, works that we at first are blind to see. It is during these times when it is most fit that we are to praise God, not curse His name. Our faith grows ever stronger in the traps we fall into when we are found not questioning God, but praising Him and thanking Him for His power and strength: His strength alone that provides the way out and will lead us there if we would but wait for His timing to reveal it.

During life's storms, we need to stop a moment and rejoice in our Lord. We need to remember the promises of comfort and hope He gives us in His Word and through His Spirit. In our Red Seas and Jordan Rivers of earthly afflictions, we still need to praise God.

"I have come down to deliver them from the Egyptians, and to bring them up out of that land to a good and broad land, a land flowing with milk and honey" (Exodus 3:8). He surely will deliver those who call on His name.

The fear of the Lord is the beginning of knowledge; fools despise wisdom and instruction. — Proverbs 1:7

The foundation and perfecting of wisdom is the fear of the Lord, without which all other knowledge is vain and useless. The beginning of wisdom is found in the temper of reverence and awe: the fear of the finite in the presence of the infinite, of the sinful in the presence of the holy.

"But the Lord takes pleasure in those who fear him, in those who hope in his steadfast love" (Psalm 147:11). Fools are individuals who have no true wisdom, who follow their own devices, without regard to reason or reverence for God: those who take "counsel without knowledge" (Job 42:3). Fools refuse to have or long for a close, intimate relationship with God. Let Divine truths and commands be to us most honorable; let us value them, and then they shall be so to us.

He was revealed in flesh, vindicated in spirit, seen by angels, proclaimed among Gentiles, believed in throughout the world, taken up in glory. — 1Timothy 3:16

-And-

And the Word became flesh and lived among us, and we have seen his glory, the glory as of a father's only son, full of grace and truth. — John 1:14

The mystery of God becoming man is to be adored, not curiously inquired upon. Let us remember that God was manifest in the flesh to take away our sins, to redeem us from all iniquity, and to purify us onto Himself. These doctrines must be shown forth by the fruits of the Spirit in our lives.

"For God has done what the law, weakened by the flesh, could not do: by sending his own Son in the likeness of sinful flesh, and to deal with sin, he condemned sin in the flesh" (Romans 8:3). The Word separates the flesh from the spirit: our carnal desires from God's desires. Jesus Christ is the embodiment of the Father's thought; He is the Word of God who was "with God in the beginning" (John 1:2). The Word came near; coming down to earth, Christ continued to share the message of the Father's love, being His voice to humanity.

"The one who rejects me and does not receive my word has a judge; on the last day the word that I have spoken will serve as judge, for I have not spoken on my own, but the Father who sent me has himself given me a commandment about what to say and what to speak" (John 12:48-49). The one who does not take Jesus' words to heart, drilling them home to their mind, and securing the truths in their soul, rejects the Father and every word of truth He speaks. Being in the flesh, let us accept the sacrifice of the One who came in the flesh to become the sacrifice for sinners so that through Him our souls will not be damned to Satan.

Great and amazing are your deeds, Lord God the Almighty! Just and true are your ways, King of the nations. — Revelation15:3

While believers stand in this world in times of trouble, as upon a sea of glass mingled with fire, they may look forward to their final deliverance, while new mercies call forth new hymns of praise. The more we know of God's wonderful works, the more we shall praise His greatness as the Lord God Almighty, the Creator and ruler of all.

Who that considers the power of God's wrath, the value of His favor, or the glory of His holiness, would refuse to fear and honor Him alone? His praise is above Heaven and earth. When the fires of affliction draw songs of praise from us, we are purified, and God is glorified. The flames that burn around us release notes of trust in God and bring cheerful compliance with His will.

Give thanks in all circumstances; for this is the will of God in Christ Jesus for you. —1 Thessalonians 5:18

Paul reminds us that we are to "Rejoice in the Lord always; again, I will say, rejoice" (Philippians 4:4). We are to give thanks in the good *and* bad times! Paul does not command us to give thanks *for* all circumstances -God knows full well that all circumstances in life will not be fitted to our favor- but *in* all of life's circumstances; this is God's will for us.

The child of Christ needs always be a joyful person, knowing that "all things work together for good for those who love God" (Romans 8:28). Christ need be our only stronghold in the bad *and* good times. What will come of our rejoicing? Peace! We shall obtain peace and further share it with a hurting world; many more souls -not simply ours alone- will know the peace of Christ.

In the last chapter of his first letter to the Thessalonians, Paul restates some God's characteristics that he, in turn, expects his brothers and sisters in Christ to obtain and perform while on earth, thus being a perfect reflection of the holy Godhead (1 Thessalonians 5:10-22). We must remain faithful, as the One who calls us is faithful.

Of course, there is great gain in godliness combined with contentment; for we brought nothing into the world, so that we can take nothing out of it. — 1Timothy 6:6-7

We learn to be content when we realize and grasp the greatest gift of contentment: eternal life with God. Spiritual contentment outstrips the value of earthly contention. We mustn't let the things of the flesh outweigh our delight taken in things of the Spirit. We learn to truly be content with our lives when all we live for is Christ, and Him glorified. We are set free -living in complete contentment- when the soul is freed from the slavery of the flesh (carnal desires and earthly longings).

Let us be as Paul, declaring: "Not that I am referring to being in need; for I have learned to be content with whatever I have. I know what it is to have little, and I know what it is to have plenty. In any and all circumstances I have learned the secret of being well-fed and of going hungry, of having plenty and of being in need" (Philippians 4:11-12). May we, with gratitude in our heart, confess that what we have and need comes from God alone, further strengthening us to work for His good pleasure.

> *Whoever comes to me and does not hate father and mother, wife and children, brothers and sisters, yes, and even life itself, cannot be my disciple.* — Luke 14:26

Hate is a harsh word. When we read this in Scripture, coming from Christ's own lips, we can't help but wonder why a loving God would ask us to go so far as hating anyone. Jesus is referring to the level of commitment we give to Him, even if that goes so far as seeming like hating another. God has required our full commitment. He must be our top priority and loved to the point that our earthly loves pale in comparison.

One that gives any person or thing preference to Christ in the affections of his heart cannot establish true discipleship; the costs must be counted and weighed out; we must be willing to surrender everything and everyone for the sake of Christ. We must proclaim as Paul did, that "I do not count my life of any value to myself, if only I may finish my course and the ministry that I received from the Lord Jesus, to testify to the good news of God's grace" (Acts 20:24). In Heaven, we will have a hundred times what we lost an entire family of believers who love Christ and who love us-. Even the material things that we had forsaken to follow Him will be given back to us in a form one hundred times better than what we had lost.

> *Rejoice in the Lord always;*
> *again I will say, Rejoice.*
> —Philippians 4:4

-AND-

> *Though the fig tree does not blossom,*
> *and no fruit is on the vines;*
> *though the produce of the olive fails,*
> *and the fields yield no food;*
> *though the flock is cut off from the fold*
> *and there is no herd in the stalls,*
> *yet I will rejoice in the Lord;*
> *I will exult in the God of my salvation.*
> —Habakkuk 3:17-1

Satan hates the sound of our rejoicing; his ears are deafened by our praise to the Lord. When we rejoice always in the Lord -even in the midst of trials- the Holy Spirit turns our sorrows into gladness. As children and "heirs of God and joint-heirs with Christ" (Romans 8:17), and as children assured that all things, even those that are the most distressing, shall work together for our good, we have sufficient reason for rejoicing always.

A sanctified soul is a living soul, and that life is peace (Philippians 4:9). Christ's children need to be called again and again to rejoicing; it more than outweighs all causes for sorrow. It is the privilege of Christ's followers to do this, not at certain periods or during distant times, but at all times we may rejoice that there is a God and Savior. We may rejoice in the character, word, and government of God, in His promises and communion with Him. Christ's children may be and should be always happy people. If everything else changes, the Lord does not. If the sources of all other joy are dried up, Christ's love and grace do not. There is not a moment of a Christian's life in which he may not find joy in the character, government, and Word of God.

Chapter 12

God's Word

Indeed, the word of God is living and active, sharper than any two-edged sword, piercing until it divides soul from spirit, joints from marrow; it is able to judge the thoughts and intentions of the heart.
— **Hebrews 4:12**

The Holy Scripture is the Word of God that was "in the beginning with God" (John 1:2). When God sets it home by the Holy Spirit, it convinces powerfully, converts powerfully, and comforts powerfully. It makes a soul that has long been proud to be humble and a perverse spirit to be meek and obedient. Sinful habits that have become natural to the soul are separated and cut off by this sword. It will discover men's thoughts and purposes, the vileness of many, the bad principles they are moved by, and the sinful ends they act to. The Word of God will show the sinner all that is in his heart.

Let us take the "helmet of salvation, and the sword of the Spirit, which is the Word of God" (Ephesians 5:17), holding fast to the divine truths in our heart, living the principles in our lives and submitting to them in our souls.

All scripture is inspired by God and is useful for teaching, for reproof, for correction, and for training in righteousness. — 2 Timothy 3:16

-And-

No prophecy ever came by human will, but men and women moved by the Holy Spirit spoke from God. — 2 Peter 1:21

The Bible is a sure guide to eternal life. The prophets and apostles did not speak from themselves but delivered what they received of God. The Scriptures are profitable for all purposes of life. Those who desire to know the things of God and be sure of them must know the Holy Scriptures; they are the divine revelation directly from God to His people, spoken through His Holy Spirit.

The Holy Word is of use to all, for all need to be taught, corrected, and reproved. There is something in the Scriptures suitable for every case, every situation, and every person. We need to love the Word of God most preciously and keep it close to our heart. Then we shall find benefit and at last, gain the happiness promised by faith in our Lord Jesus Christ.

Your word is a lamp to my feet and a light to my path.
— Psalm 119:105

God's Word keeps the feet from stumbling, as a flame burning that lights the road continually, so that we may see ahead, able to take each step without faltering. Like a torch being carried through the darkness, when the moon is hidden by clouds of doubt, pain, or grief, God's Word is our light. The light is kept burning with the oil of the Spirit, as a light to direct us in the choice of our way. We may bless God for the light shining as in a dark place, to guide us until the Son of Righteousness shall come; for Christians "will see his face, and his name will be on their foreheads. And there will be no more night; they need no light of lamp or sun, for the Lord God will be their light, and they will reign forever and ever" (Revelation 22:4-5).

The Son has come, and we may rejoice because we are given His light through the Holy Spirit, to keep our road bright in the darkened places and to guide our steps so our feet do not stumble. So, the Son has become for us this Word, this burning lamp, this torch we hold aloft that shines along the road, blinding the eyes of our enemies, and leading us always to safe destinations.

We also constantly give thanks to God for this, that when you received the word of God that you heard from us, you accepted it not as a human word but as what it really is, God's word, which is also at work in you believers. —1 Thessalonians 2:13

From the moment a believer comes to Christ, to the resurrection of the body at the end of the ages, the Father works with all the scattered material of our lives, working to shape us deeper and deeper into the image of His Son, so that when we breathe our last here on earth, we may perfectly reflect Christ.

Jesus is the embodiment of the Father's total message to humanity: the written Word of God. To reject Christ is to reject the One who sent Him and the written Word of the profits and saints that followed; hindering that Gospel is hindering the salvation of souls. The Word wrought in the Christ child makes Him an example to others in faith and good works, and for the sake of the Gospel, endures trials and is patient under suffering. We should receive the Word of God with affections suitable to its holiness, wisdom, truth, and goodness. The words of men are frail and perishing, like themselves, and sometimes false, foolish, and fickle; but God's Word is holy, wise, just, and faithful; let us receive and regard it accordingly.

> *He made my mouth like a sharp sword,*
> *in the shadow of his hand he hid me;*
> *he made me a polished arrow,*
> *in his quiver he hid me away.*
> —Isaiah 49:2

Every word spoken by the prophet is a direct message from God to His people. The very words of Christ -the Messiah- have power and authority. The sharp sword is the very words spoken by Christ, wounding the conscience of men so that their lies, lusts, and carnal desires strike them down; but all these wounds are healed when the sinner prays to Christ for grace and mercy.

Christ is also like a carefully made and polished arrow in the service of the Father, ready to be used at the right time. The arrow when fit to and released from the bowstring will fly high and swift. Christ was hidden in the Father's quiver until His ministry began. Now may that arrow strike us; not strike us down, but pierce our very soul with the truth of the Father's love, grace, and mercy through His Son, so that we, in turn, may share this Polished Arrow with others.

Chapter 13

Joy and Sorrow

Sorrow is better than laughter, for by sadness of countenance the heart is made glad. —Ecclesiastes 7:3

Look at the thorns, not just the roses God gives you. Through your tears, you will see God's rainbow after the storm. We are often content living on the outer edge of our soul; but when we live on the outside, we are never able to see the depths within -the floodgates of joy that come forth after the storms of sorrow.

Sorrow is the yielding light that slows us down; we are able to examine who we really are, who we have been made to be; furthermore, we will be more mindful of the Heavenly life, walking closer in joy with our Lord. Sorrow reveals the person inside that God has made us to be. Through the sorrows of life, we die to ourselves, awakening to the true person God has created: not living for this world but living for God's good work, plowing the grounds of His garden for a richer harvest. Think of one that never knew the crush of sorrow upon his heart; his soul would not expand to greater depths; he would not know the fruitfulness God means to set forth through a downcast spirit. Had we not known sorrow, we would not have known God's rich harvest of joy and comfort He sends forth from Heaven. Blessed is the darkness of sorrow, for it reveals God's stars that shine with the light of His joy.

God will never use anyone to a great degree until He has broken them completely. Only through sorrow is the heart humbled and the soul strengthened. "The joy of the Lord is your strength" (Nehemiah 8:10).

Therefore in the east give glory to the Lord; in the coastlands of the sea glorify the name of the Lord, the God of Israel. — Isaiah 24:15

All around, the world is filled with wickedness, wrath, deceit, and despair. Yet, the joy of God's children is as lively as ever because the covenant of grace -the fountain of their comforts, and the foundation of their hope- lie in Christ alone.

Those who rejoice in the Lord can rejoice even in the tribulations that surround them, and by faith may triumph when all about them are in tears. They encourage their fellow-sufferers to do likewise, even those who are in the furnace of affliction. In every fire, even the hottest, in every place, even the most remote, let us keep up our good thoughts of God. If none of these trials moves us, then we glorify the Lord in the fires.

The best way to show our gratitude to God is to accept everything, even our problems, with joy. — Mother Teresa

As sorrowful, yet always rejoicing; as poor, yet making many rich; as having nothing, and yet possessing everything. — 2 Corinthians 6:10

Willing obedience to the Lord comes through the circumstances that otherwise would seem lamentable if not for the grace of God active in our lives. Paul knew this: that his sole gain was in Christ alone, thus sowing the seed of faith, further rejoicing came with each soul saved by the blood of the Lamb. Like Paul, we can also commend ourselves as servants of God as we face our own afflictions, hardships, distresses, and poverty with patient endurance and rejoicing in the hope set before us.

Hatred stirs up strife, but love covers all offenses. — Proverbs 10:12

Paul reminds us that the greatest of the virtues is love (1 Corinthians 13:13). Just as the pardoning love and grace of God covers our sins against Him by the blood and righteousness of His Son, so too will the love we show one another put to sleep the offences made against us by our neighbors. Sins put to sleep, we are able to forgive our neighbor and forget that any past offence ever occurred.

Let us remember, rather, the Golden Rule and act on its virtue. However, those who know not God's love and grace are easily provoked by Satan's whisperings to cause harm to the one who causes them harm. Hatred against our neighbor is but fuel to Satan's fire. To tear one another apart by malice and revenge is just what the devil hopes to see happen: causing hatred and darkness amongst an already darkened world. But "*oft does hatred hurt itself?*"[8] Revenge sounds fair for a season but leads to no merit; there is no result worth applauding. Hatred against our neighbors becomes hatred against ourselves; the revenge we thought so just becomes revenge against our own soul. Must we live in such a way?

We needn't live in a way that brings Satan pleasure. Instead, we must look to the one who pardons our sins, and in the same way, fills our soul with that same love and grace. In place of hatred, love is set, and in place of revenge,

---

[8] Tolkein, JRR. (1997). *The Lord of the Rings: The Two Towers.* (2nd ed.). Houghton Mifflin.

grace is set. Let us reflect the actions of our Lord, acting by the same love and grace shown to us, sharing His love and grace with our neighbors.

Chapter 14

Hypocrisy

Beloved, do not believe every spirit, but test the spirits to see whether they are from God; for many false prophets have gone out into the world. —1 John 4:1

To prepare beforehand those who sought the truth, Jesus warns His followers: false messiahs and false prophets will appear and perform great signs and wonders to deceive, if possible, even the elect (Matthew 24:24).

Those who are well-acquainted with the Scriptures may, in humble dependence on divine teaching, discern those who set forth doctrines according to the apostles, and those who contradict them. The sum of revealed religion is in the doctrine concerning Christ, His person and office. The false teachers speak of the world according to its aphorisms and desires, so as not to offend carnal men. The true doctrine as to the person of the Christ, leading men from the world to God, is a mark of the Spirit of truth in opposition to the spirit of error.

What wonder is it that people of a worldly spirit should cling to those who are like themselves and suit their schemes and discourses to their corrupt taste? In reality, truth only comes from the Holy Spirit, everything else comes from evil. Believers will face false prophets because there are quite a few in the world. It is important to have a way to test which teachers and leaders are from God. John give details related to the difference between true and false teachers (1 John 4:2-6). May we cling to what is true, leaning on the strength of Jesus Christ, and be guided by the Holy Spirit so we will not be overtaken by those who oppose God.

The kingdom of heaven may be compared to someone who sowed good seed in his field; but while everybody was asleep, an enemy came and sowed weeds among the wheat, and then went away. So, when the plants came up and bore grain, then the weeds appeared as well. And the slaves of the householder came and said to him, 'Master, did you not sow good seed in your field? Where, then, did these weeds come from?' He answered, 'An enemy has done this.' The slaves said to him, 'Then do you want us to go and gather

112

them?' But he replied, 'No; for in gathering the weeds you would uproot the wheat along with them. Let both of them grow together until the harvest; and at harvest time I will tell the reapers, Collect the weeds first and bind them in bundles to be burned, but gather the wheat into my barn.' —Matthew 13:24-30

This parable represents the present and future states of Christ's Church: sisters and brothers come together as one, yet there lie hypocrites among the righteous: bad seeds sown by the enemy of this world, meaning to choke the righteous with falsehoods and deceit. Yet the deceivers of men's hearts must not be cut off; for who can truly tell them amongst the Church? The Holy Spirit alone is the reader of men's hearts and discerner of men's souls. He knows the righteous from the hypocrites: the ones who "do all their deeds to be seen by others" (Matthew 23:5), yet their heart is not hidden from God's sight. He knows they do not mean what they say; they do not practice what they preach.

"So, it will be at the end of the age. The angels will come out and separate the evil from the righteous" (Matthew 13:49). When the final judgment comes, believers shall shine forth to themselves; at the great day they shall shine forth before the entire world. They shall shine by reflection with light borrowed from the Fountain of light. Their sanctification will be made perfect, and their justification published. May we be found among that happy number!

You stiff-necked people, uncircumcised in heart and ears, you are forever opposing the Holy Spirit, just as your ancestors used to do. —Acts 7:51

The apostle warns the chief priests that although they have been circumcised in the flesh, they lacked circumcision of the heart: the baptism of the Holy Spirit and the fear and love of the Lord, which was not present in their lives. They could not hear Christ calling. Their ears refused to hear and take to heart the Word of the Lord or the Gospel messages of Christ. Despite their carnal circumcision, these men were uncircumcised in God's eyes. May we sincerely come to Christ, desiring to hear His voice in our ears, and longing for the baptism of His Spirit.

Those conflicts and disputes among you, where do they come from? Do they not come from your cravings that are at war within you? You want something and do not have it; so, you commit murder. And you covet something and cannot obtain it; so, you engage in disputes and conflicts. You do not have, because you do not ask. You ask and do not receive, because you ask wrongly, in order to spend what you get on your pleasures. Adulterers! Do you not know that friendship with the world is enmity with God? Therefore, whoever wishes to be a friend of the world becomes an enemy of God. Or do you suppose that it is for nothing that the scripture says, 'God yearns jealously for the spirit that he has made to dwell in us'? — James 4:1-5

In the preceding chapter, James explains to his readers what exactly causes the enmity and strife. Envy and selfish ambition is the road of the world's wisdom, trying to get what one wants for himself, frustrated by the people standing in his way; so they fight, quarrel, and even kill. Instead of trusting that they have a loving heavenly Father to provide in His perfect timing, worldly-minded people insist on fighting to obtain their desires. James elevates our awareness of how serious this problem is by putting a sharp label on it: adultery.

Are you following the wisdom of the world while claiming to be one of Christ's own children? If so, you're cheating on God with this world system of serving yourself first at all costs. You can't do both. We are reminded that if you make yourself a friend of the world, you make yourself an enemy of God (vs. 4). James warns us that if in our pride, we stay on that path, God will oppose us, but He will not reject us. Repentance is always possible; God always gives more grace (James 4:6). James answers for us in the following verses what we are to do to repent and come back to God (vs. 7-17).

Let us mark our soul with the Lord's wisdom, seeking to serve God, craving the wisdom from above that bears sweet fruits and brings love in the midst of strife. May envy and selfish ambition be thrown away, and peace be set in its place.

Go and cry to the gods whom you have chosen; let them deliver you in the time of your distress! — Judges 10:14

Many times, we don't realize the effect of our sins until they catch up to us; we find no gain from our acts, nor merit from our sinfulness, only vanity and shame. No gain for sin, we are but forced to turn to repentance, as Israel did (vs. 10), seeking forgiveness from the Lord. There is hope when sinners cry to the Lord for help and lament their ungodliness as well as their more open transgressions. It is necessary, in true repentance, that there be a full conviction that those things cannot help us which we have set in competition with God.

When our heart is humbled to the point of true repentance, the grace of God turns His anger to humbled compassion for His people (vs. 15-16). As the disobedience and misery of a child are a grief to a tender parent, so the

114

provocations of God's people are a grief to Him. From Him, mercy can never be sought in vain. We must submit to God's justice, with hope in His mercy. True repentance is not only for sin but also from sin. May we (the trembling sinners) cast ourselves to the mercy of God, humble ourselves under His hand, and seek deliverance from the powers of darkness. In such a way of humble repentance, may we seek to separate our hearts and minds from acts of sin, rejoicing in the mercy of God.

> *These are blemishes on your love-feasts, while they feast with you without fear, feeding themselves. They are waterless clouds carried along by the winds; autumn trees without fruit, twice dead, uprooted; wild waves of the sea, casting up the foam of their own shame; wandering stars, for whom the deepest darkness has been reserved forever.* — Jude 1:12-13

Peter also warns us against the practices of false prophets and teachers (2 Peter 2). False teachers are dreamers; they greatly defile and grievously wound the soul. These teachers are of a disturbed mind and a seditious spirit. They are twice dead when they start in the Spirit and end in the flesh; they had been once dead in their natural, fallen state; but now they are dead again by the evident proofs of their hypocrisy.

Jude warns his readers against these false teachers. He piles metaphor upon metaphor and epithet upon epithet in the effort to express his indignation and abhorrence. What happens before the winter? In autumn, trees become fruitless; they die and are uprooted. In the same way, these epithets are set to describe what happens to the ones who teach falsely within Christ's church. They bear no fruit for Christ's Kingdom; they wither away, dry up, and die, and eventually are uprooted on the day of God's judgment.

False teachers are to expect the worst punishments in this world and in that to come. They glare like meteors or shooting stars and then sink into the blackness of darkness forever. Christ's children must remain grounded, seeking to follow the path of righteousness, being guided by the Holy Spirit, which dwells deeply within each of Christ's own.

The Day of Judgment will come; God's wrath will be poured out upon those who dare oppose His Church, and the ungodly will be cast out forever. We are encouraged and reminded of "the only God our Savior, through Jesus Christ our Lord, be glory, majesty, power, and authority, before all time and now and forever. Amen" (Jude 1:25).

115

Chapter 15

The Last Stages

Lo, I will send you the prophet Elijah before the great and terrible day of the Lord comes. He will turn the hearts of parents to their children and the hearts of children to their parents, so that I will not come and strike the land with a curse.
— Malachi 4:5-6

John the Baptist preached repentance and reformation as Elijah had done. The turning of souls to God and their duty is the best preparation of them for the great and dreadful day of the Lord. John preached a doctrine that shall reach men's hearts and work a change in them; thus, he shall prepare the way for the kingdom of Heaven. Let the believer wait with patience for his release and cheerfully expect the great day when Christ shall come the second time to complete our salvation. But those who turn not to Him must expect to be smitten with a sword, with a curse. None can expect to escape the curse of God's broken law; they will never enjoy the happiness of His chosen and redeemed people unless their hearts are turned from sin, and the world to Christ and holiness. The grace of our Lord Jesus Christ be with us all.

He will also strengthen you to the end, so that you may be blameless on the day of our Lord Jesus Christ. God is faithful; by him you were called into the fellowship of his Son, Jesus Christ our Lord.
— 1 Corinthians 1:8-9

Those that wait for the coming of the Lord Jesus Christ will be kept by Him to the end, and those that are so will be blameless in the day of Christ, made so by rich and free grace. How glorious are the hopes of such a privilege: to be kept by the power of Christ, and from the power of our corruptions and Satan's temptations.

For this slight momentary affliction is preparing us for an eternal weight of glory beyond all measure. **— 2 Corinthians 4:17**

The hope of Christ's resurrection is an encouragement in our days of suffering and distress; our trials and sufferings are for the advantage of the Church, and to God's glory. The prospect of eternal life and happiness is our support and comfort. What our perception is quick to pronounce heavy and long, grievous and tedious, faith perceives to be light and but for a moment. The weight of all temporal afflictions is lightness itself, while the glory to come is a substance, weighty and lasting beyond description.

If the apostle could call his heavy and long-continued trials light and but for a moment, what must our trifling difficulties be? Faith enables us to make this right judgment of things. Unseen things are eternal, seen things are but temporary only. Let us then look away from the things which are seen; let us cease to seek for worldly advantages or to fear present distresses. Let us give due diligence to make our future happiness sure.

Now when these things begin to take place, stand up and raise your heads, because your redemption is drawing near. — Luke 21:28

Throughout chapter 21, Luke records what is to take place shortly before the ending of time and the great return of Christ, foreshadowed by Jesus Himself and spoken of earlier by many Old Testament prophets. Jesus mentions all these things so, in advance, His children may be prepared to face such events.

Although what Jesus says seems devastating, those that are one with Christ shall not fear such a day, for they can rest assured that they will be brought to their Savior's side to rest in peace for eternity. Despite the desolation, His coming shall be a glorious one; and those who are His in Heaven and on the earth may rejoice, knowing that their Savior reigns, coming once again to bring the Church to Himself for all time.

For in this tent we groan, longing to be clothed with our heavenly dwelling—if indeed, when we have taken it off, we will not be found naked. For while we are still in this tent, we groan under our burden, because we wish not to be unclothed but to be further clothed, so that what is mortal may be swallowed up by life. — 2 Corinthians 5:2-4

Upon receiving the grace and love of the Father through the sacrifice of His Son, we thus are clothed with the blood of the Lamb. When stripped of our flesh, our soul will not be found naked. Receiving God's gift of mercy, our soul will be clothed with an imperishable form, in which we await the final resurrection. Death will strip us of the clothing of flesh and all the comforts of life, as well as end all our troubles here below. But believing souls shall be clothed with garments of praise, with robes of righteousness and glory. The present graces and comforts of the Spirit are earnest of everlasting grace and comfort. Being clothed with the imperishable form given to us, we yet groan under the burden of the sinfulness of this world, lamenting the weight that drags and pulls on us. Believers in Christ may yet stay strong, finding strength in the faith they hold. Praise may always be given for the garment of comfort our soul is clothed with, awaiting the final redemption of our Lord.

As for you, always be sober, endure suffering, do the work of an evangelist, carry out your ministry fully. —2 Timothy 4:5

Notice that in the conclusion of this letter, Paul asks of Timothy to send forth his fellow brothers and sisters? May we also, in one way or another, strengthen our fellow brothers and sisters in Christ that they may go forth, proclaiming God's love and grace in Christ Jesus. As Christ commissioned us, so too are we to commission others. In Christ alone, we will be the salt of the earth and the light of the world. "But you are a chosen race, a royal priesthood, a holy nation, God's own people, in order that you may proclaim the mighty acts of him who called you out of darkness into his marvelous light" (1 Peter 2:9).

As for me, I am already being poured out as a libation, and the time of my departure has come. I have fought the good fight, I have finished the race, I have kept the faith. From now on there is reserved for me the crown of righteousness, which the Lord, the righteous judge, will give me on that day, and not only to me but also to all who have longed for his appearing. — 2 Timothy 4:6-8

Paul is quick to assure Timothy -and all of his readers- of the three goals set before him by his Maker that he had accomplished: he had fought the good fight, he had finished the race, and he had kept the faith. Each goal, in turn, is compatible with the other. Each characteristic supports and acknowledges the other; with one, there must also be set the other two.

Paul knew the death he was to die and was habitually ready for it. Namely, because his race was finished, his battles were fought, and his faith stayed strong on the firm ground of Christ. His earthly goals were accomplished; thus, he was ready to depart; he was willing and ready to die a death both satisfactory and pleasing to the Lord.

The blood of the martyrs, though not a sacrifice of atonement, yet was a sacrifice for the cause of Christ and a confirmation of the Gospel. Yet death to a good man is his release from the imprisonment of this sinful world, and his departure to the enjoyments of another world. May we also be ready when our Maker calls us home; may we be poured out as a drink offering and acceptable sacrifice to God.

He will cut off the chariot from Ephraim
and the war horse from Jerusalem;
and the battle bow shall be cut off,
and he shall command peace to the nations;
his dominion shall be from sea to sea,
and from the River to the ends of the earth. - **Zechariah 9:10**

Here begins a prophecy of the Messiah and His kingdom. The description that follows (vs. 11-17) is what shall come to pass when the Messiah comes, taking His Lordship to the ends of the earth and beyond. The prophet has his eye on the victories of the Messiah; and when He comes, the victories of the Jews and all who are called His own by the blood of Christ will be complete. Peace will be introduced by Him without conflict, thus harmonizing with the numerous parallel passages of Scripture in which peace is represented as a characteristic mark of the Messiah, when contention, war, and destruction shall cease.

May we look forward to this day with joy and gladness, bearing in mind the victories yet to be achieved by the Lord when He comes once and for all, rapturing His Beloved home to eternal peace.

Therefore prophesy, and say to them, Thus, says the Lord God: I am going to open your graves, and bring you up from your graves, O my people; and I will bring you back to the land of Israel. And you shall know that I am the Lord, when I open your graves, and bring you up from your graves, O my people. I will put my spirit within you, and you shall live, and I will place you on your own soil; then you shall know that I, the Lord, have spoken and will act, says the Lord. —Ezekiel 37:12-14

Ezekiel's prophecy is a clear intimation of the resurrection of the dead, and represents the power and grace of God in the conversion of the most hopeless sinners to Himself. Let us look to Him who will at last open our graves and bring us forth to judgment, that He may now deliver us from sin, and put His Spirit within us, and keep us by His power, through faith, unto salvation.

What I am saying, brothers and sisters, is this: flesh and blood cannot inherit the kingdom of God, nor does the perishable inherit the imperishable. Listen, I will tell you a mystery! We will not all die, but we will all be changed, in a moment, in the twinkling of an eye, at the last trumpet. For the trumpet will sound, and the dead will be raised imperishable, and we will be changed. For this perishable body must put on imperishability, and this mortal body must put

119

on immortality. When this perishable body puts on imperishability, and this mortal body puts on immortality, then the saying that is written will be fulfilled: 'Death has been swallowed up in victory.'
— 1 Corinthians 15:50-54

Paul takes this opportunity to speak to his readers of the mystery of the rapture of Jesus Christ (see also Revelation 19-22): the end of the age when Christ is to return and take His Church home. We are to put these earthly bodies aside, as they were made only from the dust of the earth, "and the dust returns to the earth" (Ecclesiastes 12:7). Heaven is a place of the imperishable, for the immortal body and soul. Immortality shall be put on, fitting us for our heavenly home.

"He will transform the body of our humiliation that it may be conformed to the body of his glory, by the power that also enables him to make all things subject to himself" (Philippians 3:21). Those in Christ shall not die, but with Him obtain victory over the grave; the risen life in Christ will taunt the death we once knew and feared: "Death has been swallowed up in victory. Where, O death, is your victory? Where, O death, is your sting?" (1 Corinthians 15:54-55). "***God's children are destined for life as resurrected bodies on a resurrected earth.***"[9]

The wine dries up, the vine languishes, all the merry-hearted sigh.
— Isaiah 24:7

This is what will come to pass when Christ returns; and all those who have stored up for themselves earthly treasures, they will dry up as sour wine, giving no delight to the one who drinks it. They will soon be brought to want and misery. There are none but the enemies of God to drink such wine. The world we live in is a world of disappointment, a vale of tears; the children of men in it are but temporary and full of trouble. See the power of God's curse, how it makes all empty and lays waste to all ranks and conditions? Sin brings these calamities upon the earth; it is polluted by the sins of man; therefore, it is made desolate by God's judgments.

Carnal joy will soon be at an end, and the end of it is the heaviness of heart. God has many ways to embitter such desires to those who love them. Let men learn to mourn for sin and rejoice in God; then no worldly desire, no treasure can take their joy from them.

---

[9] Randy A. (2004, ch.9) *Heaven.* Tyndale Momentum.

The seventh angel poured his bowl into the air, and a loud voice came out of the temple, from the throne, saying, 'It is done!'
— Revelation 16:17

Christ's work had come to fulfillment through an empty tomb. Rising again He conquered life and death; and all those that would follow Him may, for a time, have communion with the Father. Yet, when our Savior comes again, we will know it truly is done! The Spirit will fill the temple and once more cry in a loud voice, "It is done!" The curse of darkness will be broken forever. The final judgment will come to an end, and those He calls His own will be gathered to be with Him for eternity.

Sin will be consumed, not only for a time but forevermore. Satan will be destroyed, and those who followed his ways -seeking after darkness instead of finding the light- will be annihilated along with him. The Son proclaims complete communion with the Father in the midst of a sinful and fallen world; but He will come again, and when He brings His children home, His plans once and for all will be complete.

The fifth angel poured his bowl on the throne of the beast, and its kingdom was plunged into darkness; people gnawed their tongues in agony. — Revelation 16:10

When Christ took His seat upon His throne, Satan and his kingdom were destroyed, for a time; none who came to be one with Christ would be touched by Satan's attacks without Christ's counsel or hands upon their heart, guiding their way by the Holy Spirit.

When Christ comes again to set His feet upon this earth and to bring His righteous ones home, Satan ("the beast") and his kingdom will be destroyed, not only for a time but forever. Let sinners now seek for Christ and the grace of the Holy Spirit, or they will have the anguish and horror of an un-humbled, impenitent, and desperate heart, thus adding to their guilt and misery; they, along with their master, will be no more.

The wolf and the lamb will feed together, and the lion will eat straw like the ox; but the serpent—its food shall be dust! They shall not hurt or destroy on all my holy mountain, says the Lord. — Isaiah 65:25

In the new Heaven and new earth (which Isaiah speaks of as God's remedy to bring a rebellious people back to Himself), all shall live in harmony and perfect peace with one another. The inclination of sinners shall be completely mortified.

121

The Church on earth shall be filled with happiness like that of Heaven. The harm, pain, and suffering that once was felt will no longer be remembered or renewed. Those who are the servants of God -who are crucified with Christ- may rest assured knowing that the time draws near for this new Heaven and new earth to come to fulfillment, wherein God's servants will live in perfect peace and enjoyment in all that is necessary for our happiness. In those happy days, all shall feed on the same spiritual food, and all shall find refreshment by the Word of God, fulfilled forever through His Son. As workers together with God, let us attend His ordinances and obey His commands, that the harmony to come upon a fallen world may be one obtained in this life.

> *For the Lord himself, with a cry of command, with the archangel's call and with the sound of God's trumpet, will descend from heaven, and the dead in Christ will rise first. Then we who are alive, who are left, will be caught up in the clouds together with them to meet the Lord in the air; and so, we will be with the Lord forever.*
> — 1 Thessalonians 4:16-17

This day is to come as a "thief in the night" (1 Thessalonians 5:2). Not knowing when the mighty day of the Lord is to come upon mankind, yet we wait eagerly for such a day, knowing that Christ will take us home. Paul speaks comfort for the family and friends of those who die in the Lord. We may weep for our own loss, though it may be their gain. Yet we must not be excessive in our sorrows; this is too much like those who have no hope of a better life.

Death is an unknown thing, and we know little about the state after death, yet the doctrines of Scripture, the resurrection and the second coming of Christ make for a remedy against the fear of death, and undue sorrow for the death of our Christian brothers and sisters; and of these doctrines, we have full assurance. It will be some happiness that Christ's children shall meet and remain together forever; but the principal happiness of Heaven is to be with the Lord, to see Him, live with Him, and enjoy Him forever. Many fear death; they know not of the afterlife; they know not where their soul will be at rest. Despite the unknown state after death, we can live assured that at Christ's second coming, He will take His faithful followers to be with Him forever; their soul will rest in Christ.

> *That the creation itself will be set free from its bondage to decay and will obtain the freedom of the glory of the children of God. We know that the whole creation has been groaning in labor pains until now; and not only the creation, but we ourselves, who have the first*

fruits of the Spirit, groan inwardly while we wait for adoption, the redemption of our bodies. — Romans 8:21-23

The soul being redeemed by the blood of the Lamb, we now wait with longing for the redemption of the body, in which the mortal will be swallowed up by this life. We remain now, but spiritually reborn, knowing only the faith held strong in our soul. Hereafter will be the coming of our physical rebirth. Those that know not Christ's love live in fear of such a day: having a baron soul, neither washed clean by Christ's blood nor restored to a new creation by the faith we hold. Their soul being reborn to nothing, thus their bodies, when dead on this earth, shall remain so; they will know not the joy of having the resurrection of life everlasting. God's children needn't fear but rather look forward to such a day with joy and gladness in their hearts. We wait for the revealing of Christ to come again, that we may live eternally as resurrected bodies on a resurrected earth.

Then he said to me, 'It is done! I am the Alpha and the Omega, the beginning and the end. To the thirsty, I will give water as a gift from the spring of the water of life. Those who conquer will inherit these things, and I will be their God and they will be my children.' — Revelation 21:6-7

The One from the throne speaks, not of the current Heaven and earth (which are fulfilled in the book of Genesis and proclaimed in Psalm 33:6-9), but of the eternal, everlasting creation of the new Heaven and new earth, "coming down out of heaven from God" (v. 10). Those who thirst for spiritual satisfaction find that Jesus Christ gives it without charge. His grace saves and satisfies the thirsting soul.

During His earthly ministry, Jesus told a spiritually thirsty woman at Jacob's well: "But those who drink of the water that I will give them will never be thirsty. The water that I will give will become in them a spring of water gushing up to eternal life" (John 4:14). The fourth beatitude promises that those "who hunger and thirst for righteousness, for they will be filled" (Matthew 5:6). That promise is fulfilled in eternity. Jesus' spoken words of creating all things new will come to fulfillment. He affirms that what He began has come to pass (thus always finishing what He began). Christ's children have something very rich, pleasurable, and satisfactory to look forward to. May the sanctifying consolations of the Holy Spirit prepare us for this heavenly happiness.

Then I saw a new heaven and a new earth; for the first heaven and the first earth had passed away, and the sea was no more. And I saw the holy city, the new Jerusalem, coming down out of heaven from

God, prepared as a bride adorned for her husband. And I heard a loud voice from the throne saying, 'See, the home of God is among mortals. He will dwell with them as their God; they will be his peoples, and God himself will be with them.' — Revelation 21:1-3

The Father foretold through the prophet Isaiah, "For I am about to create new heavens and a new earth; the former things shall not be remembered or come to mind" (Isaiah 65:17). Upon receiving such grace given to us, our mind is thus set on the life beyond this earth: the new Heaven and earth, freed from the vanity to which things present are subject, and the sin we are polluted with. Those only who are clothed with the righteousness of Christ and sanctified by the Holy Spirit will be there: those whose names are "written in the Lamb's book of life" (Revelation 21:27) shall be admitted to dwell in this holy place.

Heaven shall become earth incarnate, just as Christ is God incarnate; Heaven and earth shall become one, thus fulfilling God's long-delayed plan to bring humanity to Himself (John 14:3, Ephesians 1:10, 2 Peter 3:13). Those who hold themselves prisoners of Christ are headed for a better life. Christ's children should be always of one mindset, focusing on one eternal goal: "the heavenly call of God in Christ Jesus" (Philippians 3:14). And when this day comes, the Lord's children shall be with Him *forever!* "**We were made for a person and a place: Jesus is the person; Heaven is the place.**"[10]

They will see his face, and his name will be on their foreheads. — Revelation 22:4

When the time comes for Christ to set foot upon this earth once more, to come and take His Church home to Himself, He will be exposed in all His glory. Until the time Christ came, no one had seen God; He is only to be seen through the Lord Jesus Christ. Those who are His shall see Him as He is, through the very face of Christ; and the names of each child of God (who have been baptized in the blood of the Lamb) will have His name written upon them for eternity, declaring none other than their belonging to God alone. The pure in heart shall see Him (Matthew 5:8).

In the revelation given to John, unbelievers receive the mark of the beast on their foreheads as a pledge of their loyalty to him (Revelation 13:16–17). It will be so at the end of time; however, the ones that belong to Christ alone shall receive His name written forever upon their forehead: an everlasting sign of loyalty and love to the One true God. Believers shall be known as sons and daughters of God to all the citizens of the New Jerusalem, so that

[10] Randy A. (April,2004). *Heaven.* Tyndale Momentum.

the free flow of mutual love among the members of Christ's family will be known to all.

ABOUT
KHARIS PUBLISHING

KHARIS PUBLISHING is an independent, traditional publishing house with a core mission to publish impactful books, and channel proceeds into establishing mini-libraries or resource centers for orphanages in developing countries, so these kids will learn to read, dream, and grow. Every time you purchase a book from Kharis Publishing or partner as an author, you are helping give these kids an amazing opportunity to read, dream, and grow. Kharis Publishing is an imprint of Kharis Media LLC. Learn more at

https://www.kharispublishing.com.

CPSIA information can be obtained
at www.ICGtesting.com
Printed in the USA
BVHW031859250221
600588BV00011B/6/J